THE INCREDIBLE SHRINKING GOSPEL

LEE WYATT

Energion Publications
Gonzalez, FL 32560
2015

ISBN10: 1-63199-216-3
ISBN13: 978-1-63199-216-2
Library of Congress Control Number: 2015950261

Energion Publications
P. O. Box 841
Gonzalez, FL 32560

energion.com
pubs@energion.com
850-525-3916

TABLE OF CONTENTS

Dedicated to my beloved wife Carolyn who has endured more than any wife should and done it with such grace that it is from her that I have truly experienced God's unconditional love.

PART I: THE CRISIS

CHAPTER I

THE CRISIS OF EVANGELISM IN THE 21ST CENTURY

THE CRISIS

The church in North America has been having a "terrible, horrible, no good, very bad day"[1] for more than forty years now! We're losing members, are biblically illiterate, and short on credibility. Even our bell-weather mega-church, Willow Creek, has recently confessed that despite its numbers and activities, it has not succeeded in growing mature disciples!

What's gone wrong? Esteemed theologian Stanley Hauerwas hits the nail on the head when he says that the church in our time has managed to do the impossible: make the gospel boring and God irrelevant to our lives.[2] No surprise, then, that our message has become unintelligible and unappealing to those outside the church. These are the folks we want to reach for God, yet the present state and confusion of the church makes it increasingly difficult to do that.

Our default response to this crisis has been to call for evangelism, evangelism, and more evangelism. Yet, what if the way we do (or don't do) evangelism is not the real problem? What if that puts the cart before the horse? Don't we need to first revisit the message we seek to share through evangelism? What if it's that message itself

---

1 Judith Viorst, *Alexander and the Terrible, Horrible, No Good, Very Bad Day* (Aladdin, 1987).

2 Stanley Hauerwas, "Preaching as Though we Had Enemies," First Things May (1995) at http://www.firstthings.com/article/2008/09/003-preaching-as-though-we-had-enemies--9: "God has entrusted us, God's church, with the best story in the world. With great ingenuity we have managed to make the story, with the aid of much theory, boring has hell.'"

that leaves folks cold and untouched? If so, then no matter how motivated we are or how well we do evangelism we will likely still meet mostly with yawns of indifference or even hostile rejection. I believe this is precisely our dilemma. We must first ask ourselves: What is the "Gospel," (the "Evangel" of evangelism)?

Vincent van Gogh experienced this firsthand and pictured it in his wonderful painting *Starry Night* (see below).

Bold yellow is Vincent's color for life and vitality. Indeed it is his way of testifying to presence of God! With that in mind, look carefully at the painting. What is the only structure that has no light in any of its windows? The Church!

As a young man Van Gogh took a temporary post as a missionary in the coal-mining district of Borinage in Belgium. He sought to serve these wretched poor as he believed Jesus would have, living with and among them rather than in the far nicer official church missionary quarters. He shared their hardships and joys, experienced life as they did, even to the point of sleeping on straw in a small hut in the rear of the village baker's house.

This kind of radical solidarity with the people was too much for Vincent's church's leaders however. Appalled at his lack of respect for the "dignity" of the office of priest, Vincent was dismissed. From that day forward Vincent rejected both the "gospel" and the institutions of the established church. "That God of the clergyman, he is to me as dead as a doornail," he wrote. And he accused the ministry of the institutional church of "icy coldness." He found abundant evidence of God alive and well in the world of nature and humanity but no longer in the church. Vincent considered himself "no friend of present-day Christianity."[3]

Vincent's experience is a forerunner of today's numerous complaints about a similarly limited and limiting "gospel." Obviously there's more askew here than simply the way we do evangelism!

OVERVIEW OF THE INCREDIBLE SHRINKING GOSPEL

It is my thesis that we in North America are in fact operating with a decidedly deficient "gospel." I call it the "Incredible Shrinking Gospel"! And I mean "incredible" in two senses. First, it seems unbelievable to me that as God's people we have so easily settled for so little of what God has given us to share with his world! And secondly, the little of what God has given us to share that we have tried to present has grown increasingly unbelievable or irrelevant to world we seek for God's sake. This tragedy will not be reversed until we take a fresh look at the "gospel" we have been given to share and that new vision of the content of the gospel inspires and shapes our efforts to share it with the world.

In "Part 1: The Crisis" I will explore in Chapter 1 the tragedy of this "shrinking" gospel in more detail and introduce a perspective that helps me analyze the gospel and identify elements we need to recover and rethink. In Chapter 2 we'll look at the differences between the biblical gospel and our "shrunken" version.

---

3   Cited in Skye Jethani, *The Divine Commodity: Discovering a Faith Beyond Consumer Christianity* (Grand Rapids: Zondervan, 2009), 10.

Part 2: Revisiting Jesus explores and clarifies essential terms in evangelism: "Empire"[4] (Chapter 3) and "gospel" (Chapter 4). In succeeding chapters we will follow Jesus and his Empire-centered ministry as he defines his read the lore of Israel's story as the plot line for his ministry (Chapter 5), his core or creed by which he declared and embodied the meaning and purpose of human life (Chapter 6), the corps he needs to fulfill his mission as demonstrated in his ministry (Chapter 7), the more of God's love climaxing in his bleed (death and resurrection) and the reconciliation flowing from it which exceeds our imagination (Chapter 8), the spore who are his seed as his family going forth in his name and for his purposes (Chapter 9), and the store of resources he provides as his feed, the primary form of his continuing presence with and nourishment for his people (Chapter 10). A summary chapter, The Jesus Deed(Chapter 11) will pull all the strands together. This material will provide us with the baseline we need to reframe our understanding of the gospel and point to ways to share it in our time and place.

The book concludes in Part 3: Revisiting Evangelism with "Whither Evangelism? The Gospel of the Empire in the 21st Century" (Chapter 12), and two chapters expounding a new view of evangelism, "And so . . . (Chapters 13-14). A Postscript closes the book with further concluding reflections.

My thesis, to repeat, is that we have a crisis in evangelism that stems ultimately from a truncated grasp of the "gospel" we find in the biblical story, and that in two senses. First, in terms of the biblical story itself, we have forgotten, ignored, or left out the very last scene of that story – the one that gives us the fullest picture, largest context, and most comprehensive meaning of what God is doing

---

4   "Empire" is my term for "kingdom of God." I use it because of the
     current interest in American "Empire" and to insist that biblically the
     kingdom of God is every bit as much a tangible, political, earthly sover-
     eignty as the American Empire (as we will see throughout the rest of this
     book).

with us and our world and where he is taking us. If we don't know how the story really ends its hard to follow the story line right.[5]

From this it follows, secondly, that the "gospel" we offer the world in Jesus' name is inevitably distorted and diluted. It can (and does) more easily fall prey to the "isms" and "ologies" that confront and contest it in the world.[6] Worst of all, such a diluted and diminished "gospel" can even become a fashionable falsification of what the gospel truly is.

We will focus on Jesus' ministry for both fundamental and strategic reasons. Fundamental, because Jesus is the key figure, the central clue to the entire biblical drama. He is the gospel in human flesh. It stands to reason that what he says and does will give us our best entrée into the meaning and significance of God's work from creation onwards. In other words, we will go right to the source to get the meaning of the gospel straight.

Our consideration of Jesus' ministry is also strategic. Oddly, his ministry as we find it in our canonical gospels suffers considerable neglect in North American churches at present. Conservative churches tend to find their theological center in a view of Paul and his teaching largely shaped by the issues of the Reformation in the 16th century rather than the 1st century Jewish setting he actually lived in. Thus they work out their theology in a rather surprising neglect of the gospels.[7] There is nothing wrong with Paul, of course, understood in his own setting. But he himself, by his own testimony, builds on the foundation which is Christ (1 Corinthians 3:10-11). So I believe we ought to return to that (oft neglected) foundation ourselves.

Liberal churches focus more on Jesus but tend to treat him largely as a moral example and inspiration for our own efforts to

---

5   There are many ways we could demonstrate this shrinkage of the gospel in the biblical material. I focus here primarily on the forgotten last scene of the story because it directly addresses the issues needing to be faced and does so in a way especially pertinent to the focus of this study.

6   More on these "isms" and "ologies" in Chapter 2.

7   N. T. Wright, "The Cross and the Caricatures" at http://www.fulcrum-anglican.org.uk/news/2007/20070423wright.cfm?doc=205.

be faithful Christians in the world. But surely the Jesus we meet in the gospels is much more than, though certainly not less than, a moral example for us to follow. This reading misses the fullness and depth of the drama of the Jesus story.[8] Thus, a rereading of the Jesus story certainly seems in order.

THE GOSPEL-CULTURE-CHURCH TRIANGLE[9]

There has been a tendency through church history, and especially in our own time and place, to identify the church and the gospel. We assume there is an unproblematic relation between church and gospel and that the two together in concert seek to address and change the culture. In other words, we have a straight line relation:

Gospel/Church ---------------- Culture

This was never true, of course, but it has become crystal clear in our own time that the church often can, and does, stray far from the gospel and impacts the world in ways that betray rather than reflect the gospel. Indeed, the church itself needs continual reformation by the gospel. The old reformed slogan from the 16th and 17th century, *Ecclesia Reformata, Semper Reformanda* ("the Church reformed, always being reformed"), says it well. Reformed, yes, God has worked in us to bring us to himself and set us on his way. Yet we always need continuing reformation because in ignorance and/

---

8   I think here of John Dominic Crossan's, *The Historical Jesus: The Life of a Mediterranean Jewish Peasant* (HarperOne, 1993) as among the best of this genre. Yet one can hardly miss how much of the biblical story gets left out in his retelling of Jesus as a wandering Cynic sage, pungently challenging his society with pithy aphorism to lead them to greater openness and justice.

9   This Gospel-Culture-Church triangle is drawn from the work of Lesslie Newbigin. See the discussion of this "Newbigin Triangle" in George R. Hunsberger, "The Newbigin Gauntlet," The Church Between Gospel & Culture, eds. George R. Hunsberger and Craig Van Gelder (Grand Rapids: Wm. B. Eerdmans Publishing Co., 1996), 8-9. This article can also be found online at http://www.tyndale.ca/sem/inministry/viewpage.php?pid=61.

or willfulness we do not know what we should do and do not do what we know. When we lose our sense of this need for continuing reformation, we stand in danger of assuming and acting as if we stand shoulder to shoulder with God looking out at a world still not-yet-fully-redeemed.

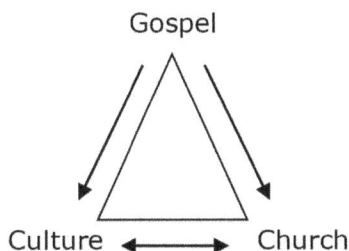

Gospel

Culture ⟷ Church

Rather than a straight-line view we ought to think in terms of a triangle. The two downward arrows from God indicate that God is at work redeeming both the church and the world at the same time. Neither stands on completely on God's side. That old reformed slogan is right: "The church, reformed (that is, in right relation to God through Jesus), always being reformed (that is, God is always working to smooth out our rough edges and tie together our loose ends so we look more and more like Christ).

The dual directional arrow running between Culture and Church means that God is at work in both of them in a way that each can and should discover his presence in the other and learn from each other to better know and discern God's presence in the world. God certainly speaks through the Church to the Culture and vice versa.

This triangle reflects what we would expect to be the case if we take incarnation of Jesus, his coming as one of us, seriously. Contrary to the widespread dualism which claims that the inner, immaterial, eternal, "spiritual" aspect of reality is superior to the (apparently) negative, dispensable material and physical aspect of reality (more on this in Chapter 2), the incarnation of Jesus shows how much God values and respects the material creation. God does not call his people away from the material world but instead fully enters it himself to seek and save his people for life as he intended it in that very world. Further,

- ✓ Jesus' bodily resurrection,
- ✓ his ascension to heaven in his human body, and
- ✓ his promise to return bodily to live with us on a new and fully material creation,

confirm the supreme worth and eternal significance of the material creation. Thus we should expect God to be at work in both Culture and Church in a mutually reciprocal fashion as our triangle indicates.

Let's rename the triangle in the terms we will be using. Let's call the "Gospel" – "The Unshrunk Gospel." And we'll call "Church" – "Church: The Incredible Shrinking Gospel." "Culture" we'll expand to "Culture/World"

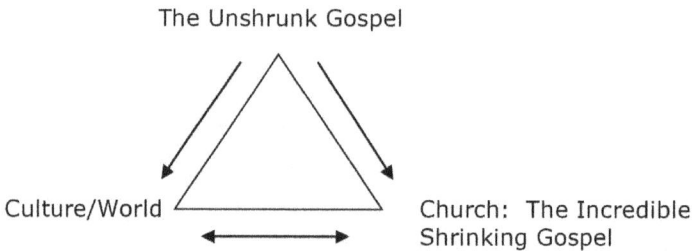

The Unshrunk Gospel

Culture/World   Church: The Incredible
                              Shrinking Gospel

The Gospel is at work even at this moment in the still not-yet-fully-redeemed world seeking to judge sin, nurture life and beauty, and set right what is unjust and oppresses God's creatures, especially the last and the least among them. The gospel is also at work in the Church, a body perennially tempted by the lures and compromises enabled by an "Incredible Shrinking Gospel." We never see far enough or practice the truth we know in a way that fully reflects God's love and passion to redeem his creation. Sometimes we even live out a "faith" that obscures and contradicts the gospel in substantial ways! Whether from the limitations of finitude or liability to arrogance and sin, the Church continually needs to be reformed by the gospel itself. Sometimes that reformation will come through the people's fresh openness to God's Word and will. Sometimes that reformation comes through a humbling, even embarrassing, awareness that our culture and our world sometimes see and act more clearly in line with God's intention for his creation than his own people do. Engagement with the gospel, the "Unshrunk Gospel," means ongoing and never-ending involvement and give and take with the cultures and world in which we live.

Now for a closer look at this "Incredible Shrinking Gospel," let's turn to Chapter 2.

THE INCREDIBLE SHRINKING GOSPEL

What I am calling "The Incredible Shrinking Gospel," got that way by virtue of both a "shrunken" biblical story and, in consequence, a truncated theology. Somewhat Esau-like, we have "despised (our) birthright" (the biblical gospel) in favor of tasty "red stuff" (the incredible shrinking gospel) that promises to slake our immediate hunger but will leave us thirsting to eat again very soon.

The Biblical Story

Here are the six "acts" of the biblical story:

1. Creation
2. Catastrophe (Sin)
3. Covenant (Israel)
4. Christ (Messiah)
5. Church
6. Consummation (Heaven/Judgment/New Creation)

While many might acknowledge that this is what the Bible teaches and the church confesses, in practice the very last scene of the last act ("New Creation") regularly gets neglected. This is easy to verify. If you ask ten people what they hope for after death, in my experience, at least nine out of ten of them who believe in life after death will respond to go to heaven and be with God or live on in some disembodied spiritual state. In other words, heaven followed by the Last Judgment is taken to be the end of the story. The New Creation, the very last scene, is left off. This, I suggest, is our *de facto* version of this last act in the biblical drama. This *de facto* version, however, not only fails to adequately reflect the biblical version, it shrinks the impact of the whole story and each of its parts.

Much of this "shrinkage" of the gospel is due to Plato. Yes, that Plato – the ancient Greek philosopher! His influential philosophy was not only the context in which the early church preached its gospel, it also shaped the content of that message in decisive ways. Some aspects of Plato's message were helpful. Others, however, ill-suited the gospel and "shrunk" the biblical message. Chief among the "shrinking" agents is Plato's pervasive dualism. This dualism has inflicted much damage to the content and presentation of the gospel in the western world.

What is dualism? It's the division of reality into two kinds: material and spiritual. The former is considered the inferior, and often negative, dimension of physicality and "stuff" that tends to weighs us down and keeps us earth-bound. Entangled in such materiality, we are unable to gain the knowledge or practice the disciplines that would free us to ascend into that better and blessed realm of the spiritual. Indeed, Plato saw the body as the prison house of the soul, from which death freed the (immortal) soul to flee back to its true, immaterial, spiritual home.

Much Christian thought, both scholarly and popular, concerning this last scene of the biblical story is heavily colored by this kind of dualistic thinking. Do not most Christians you know conceive of the last chapter of their personal story as life after death in heaven in some sort of disembodied, "spiritual" state?[10] Do not most Easter sermons you have heard trumpet the victory of the resurrection of Jesus from the dead as the assurance of just this kind of life after death? Is not the chief consolation offered at most funerals that the departed is now with God in heaven enjoying his or her eternal reward?

Two familiar hymns make this point well.[11] In Charles Wesley's *Love Divine, All Loves Excelling*, stanza 4 reads:

---

10   John Drane, *After McDonaldization: Mission, Ministry, and Christian Discipleship in an Age of Uncertainty* (Grand Rapids: Baker Academic, 2008) writes, "For generations now, the Western world (and therefore Christian theology) has been obsessed with life after death, and that still tends to feature in most, if not all, presentations of the Gospel." (87-88)

11   I owe reference to these hymns to N. T. Wright in a lecture.

Finish, then, Thy new creation; Pure and spotless let us be.
Let us see Thy great salvation Perfectly restored in Thee;
Changed from glory into glory, <u>Till in heaven we take our place,</u>
<u>Till we cast our crowns before Thee, Lost in wonder, love, and</u>
<u>praise.</u>[12]

The underlined portion reflects our traditional, dualistical-ly-tinged view which stops short of the full biblical story and our true Christian hope.

Contrast the final stanzas of Maltbie Babcock's *This is My Father's World*:

This is my Father's world.
O let me ne'er forget That though the wrong seems oft so strong,
God is the ruler yet.
<u>This is my Father's world: the battle is not done;</u>
<u>Jesus who died shall be satisfied, And earth and heaven be one.</u>[13]

Again, the underlined portion makes the point. It reflects the full biblical hope that earth and heaven shall finally be (re)united, as in the beginning, though far exceeding and excelling that beginning (a point to which we shall return). That's the real last scene in the biblical drama: a creation fully at one, God and humanity, body and spirit, humanity and creation, the physical and the spiritual – life at long last lived as God intended it in the beginning!

God's creation project will not be scrapped and done away with to be replaced be a bodiless, immaterial life presumed to be superior to the earthly, bodily life we know here. That, again, is Plato – not the Bible! The Bible, rather, envisions that we will finally know and experience life as God created it and intended it on an earth rescued, restored, and renewed to be our eternal home.[14]

---

12 "Love Divine, All Loves Excelling," *The Presbyterian Hymnal: Hymns, Psalms, and Spiritual Songs* (Louisville: Westminster John Knox Press, 1990), 376.

13 "This is My Father's World," *The Presbyterian Hymnal: Hymns, Psalms, and Spiritual Songs* (Louisville: Westminster John Knox Press, 1990), 293.

14 See Isaiah 65:17-25; Matthew 6:10; Romans 4:13; 8:18-28; 1 Corinthians 15; Revelation 21-22.

When I realized this, a question I had long pondered received its answer. That question was "Why does God leave us here to struggle and suffer after we have come to faith? If the point is to get to heaven, and we are assured by God's promises that such is indeed by faith our destiny, why all the rest?"

Why not zip us off to heaven to our reward immediately? Maybe it's to fulfill the so-called Great Commission (Matthew 28:16-20), though few Christians and churches act as though this is a compelling concern![15]

Perhaps it's that we need to grow and mature in preparation for our life in heaven. If life there, however, is a dis-embodied, "spiritual" affair it is hard to imagine how what happens to us here, discontinuous as it is believed to be with our life in heaven, can prepare us for that life. And if God is going to perfect us all in the end, why bother?

But what if our embodied existence here is to be transformed, not into a dis-embodied, "spiritual" life, but rather to a more fully embodied one?[16] What if our continued existence here as God's people is a preview, a foretaste, a demonstration, of life as we will know it when "heaven and earth are one"? What if the life we will know fully then and there, we already begin to experience in partial and fragmentary ways here and now? And what if we are the prototype, as it were, of life in God's Empire? Then:

- ✓ wooing and reaching others for Christ,
- ✓ erecting signposts of justice, mercy, and peace through our work in God's world,
- ✓ standing in solidarity with the sick and suffering, and

15 Carl Raschke, blogging at "the church and postmodern culture: conversation" (www.churchandpomo.typepad.com.conversation) on July 29, 2008 writes: "One of the problems that the contemporary, Western, 'postmodern' Christian has - which their counterparts, particularly in the global South, don't have - is that their Christianity is not really informed by the Great Commission. Western Christianity, especially in both a modern and post-modern venue, can best be described as *The Great Option*."

16 In *The Great Divorce*, C. S. Lewis pictures humans as becoming more and more real as they draw closer and begin to experience life in heaven. More real – all that they were plus much more!

✓ announcing to the world the truly "good news" of God's great and gracious plans for this world and us creatures,

already embodies and invites others to the experience of the life of the age to come,[17] that is, God's new creation of all things through Jesus Christ. And the point of the whole biblical drama comes into focus as God's seeking, finding, and saving a people who will even now begin to live out that salvation - the kind of life promised in the New Creation - in the midst of the old creation! And that's why God leaves us here, it's right where we belong!

It's as if the center of gravity in the biblical plot line shifts from the shrunken end, where traditional Christianity has it, to the center, where the Bible has it, in Jesus Christ and through him the life and ministry of his followers. Our lives and life together are through him thus invested with eternal significance. God never intended us to simply "mark time" till we die or Christ returns, hoping to save as many "souls" as we can out of the world as we go. No, God intends us here and now to begin to live as the vanguard of the New Creation – to be sign, steward, and sacrament of his Empire:

✓ a sign so the world will know God's Empire is here and also to come in its fullness and God has included the world in what he is doing;

✓ a steward so the world can see what God's Empire looks like in real life; and

---

17 This language of the "life of the age to come" is what John means by "eternal life" – his characteristic language for Matthew, Mark, and Luke's, the "Empire of Heaven/God" or Paul's "salvation." The fascinating thing about "eternal life" is, just like the other gospel writers and Paul, in John it is predominately spoken of in the present tense! This gift of the life of the age to come is a gift we begin to experience here and now in the present. Since we will be working mainly from Matthew, Mark, and Luke, I wanted to note here that John's different way of telling Jesus' story and his different way of reporting Jesus' speaking moves in the same direction as the others. Check it out!

✓   a sacrament so the world can feel, touch, and taste God's Empire for themselves.

It is for this we have been saved and to this privilege and responsibility which we must bend our bodies and souls, today, tomorrow, and every tomorrow God grants till his Empire, his New Creation, comes in its fullness!

The fullness of that Empire/New Creation experienced as the genuine last scene of the biblical drama features the cleansing, purification, and transformation of the creation which sprang from God's creative Word at the beginning, into what it was always meant to be. Not that we can truly imagine God's New Creation! It's beyond anything we can now envision! But we can anticipate its surprise and wonder in the sure hope that in its splendor and glory we will find that this New Creation is just right for us.

The New Creation sheds its transforming light backward from the future to illumine and empower us to live now as who we will be then. This accounts for our distinctiveness as God's people and for the sure and certain hope that anchors us. And it is this New Creation, not heaven (as we traditionally envision it)[18] that is our eternal destiny!

Another often overlooked feature of this gospel is articulated by the Apostle Paul in 1 Corinthians 3:10-15:

> *According to the grace of God given to me, like a skilled master builder I laid a foundation, and someone else is building on it. Each builder must choose with care how to build*

18   Is it possible to consider "heaven" as the New Testament analogue to the Old Testament's "Sheol"? The latter is not Hell or a place of judgment but rather a "holding station" for the dead who await whatever God might yet do with them. Though they had no developed ideas of an afterlife until late in the period, it seems the Old Testament writers could not accept that death was the final chapter of God's story for them. Thus, Sheol offered them breathing room, time for clearer ideas of an afterlife to develop. Heaven, it seems to me, plays a similar role, only in a setting where ideas of afterlife are well-developed. Both are "holding stations" for the dead as they await the next chapter in God's story. Though heaven, to be sure, is pictured as a much more pleasant and desirable place than Sheol!

on it. ¹¹For no one can lay any foundation other than the one that has been laid; that foundation is Jesus Christ. ¹²Now if anyone builds on the foundation with gold, silver, precious stones, wood, hay, straw — ¹³the work of each builder will become visible, for the Day will disclose it, because it will be revealed with fire, and the fire will test what sort of work each has done. ¹⁴If what has been built on the foundation survives, the builder will receive a reward. ¹⁵If the work is burned, the builder will suffer loss; the builder will be saved, but only as through fire.

Do you hear what Paul says here? You can take it with you! The normal use of this saying as a warning against chasing improper desires and goals in life, while true enough, tends to be extended to mean that ultimately nothing we do here on earth carries over to our life after death. But Paul says otherwise! The life we have fashioned in and through and for Jesus Christ here will be tested by God's refining fire (i.e. judgment[19]) and, if built by faith through grace and in love ("gold, silver, precious stones"), will be taken up by God, purified of the sin which still clings to it,[20] and used by him in the New Creation. Even if our lives and works fail utterly to pass this judgment, we will still be saved, though perhaps embarrassingly "naked," with nothing to show for our journey through this life.

---

19 Our too Protestant sensibilities combined with the "can't take it with you" mentality, overlook this judgment of our works in our commendable zeal to preserve God's grace as the basis of our acceptance and salvation. Paul, however, affirms, indeed insists on this judgment, both here and elsewhere. Our salvation is secured by grace. Our lives and works, on the other hand, await this other divine scrutiny.

20 Even our best and most faithful efforts on God's behalf are tainted by our sinfulness. This is what the grim-sounding reformed teaching, "Total Depravity," was intended to mean. It's not that we and everything we do are as bad as they could be, but rather that everything (hence "total"), even the very best we do, is tainted by our pride and self-seeking, or our withdrawal into security and comfort. These remaining taints of sin are what God's refining fire remove in this judgment of works before being used by God as building blocks of the New Creation.

In sum, we can picture the difference between the Bible's gospel and what I call the "Incredible Shrinking Gospel" like this:

Biblical Gospel	Incredible Shrinking Gospel
1. Creation	1. Creation
2. Catastrophe (Sin)	2. Catastrophe (Sin)
3. Covenant (Israel)	3. Covenant (Israel)
4. Christ (Messiah)	4. Christ (Messiah)
5. Church	5. Church
6. Consummation — Heaven — Judgment — New Creation	6. Consummation — Heaven — Judgment —

An old spiritual sings:

"This world is not my home, I'm just passing through.
My treasures are laid up somewhere beyond the blue."

As understandable as this was on the lips of oppressed slaves (and I mean them no critique here), on the lips of dualistic western Christians, it articulates this "shrunken" view of the gospel I am contesting. We could rephrase it though to reflect the true gospel perspective:

"Heaven's not my home, I'm just passing through,
Won't you wait with me for God's new creation too?"[21]

Theology

Anti-Sacramentalism

This dualistically-infected version of the gospel not only shrinks the biblical story as a whole, it shrinks key aspects of its

---

21 Or, in the title of David Lawrence's book, *Heaven is Important, But it's Not the End of the World.* Since writing this chapter, I discovered a similar treatment of this spiritual in Chris Wright, *The God I Don't Understand* (Grand Rapids: Zondervan, 2008), 194.

teaching too. This results from dualism's anti-sacramental thrust. "Sacramental" refers to God's using material and physical reality to make himself known to us. A sacramental outlook brings together what we, under dualism's influence, tend to hold apart – the spiritual and the physical. A sacramental outlook finds what we call the spiritual and the physical as complementary aspects of the one reality called life. God uses both in tandem to communicate and share his life with us. God declared the material of the created world to be "very good"; sanctified it by becoming human and journeying with us in Jesus of Nazareth; vindicated and blessed it forever in Jesus' "bodily" resurrection from the dead. Moreover, God promises to us a life forever with him in a New Creation, more real but not less physical or material than creation as we know it.

A theology that denies or fails to grasp the importance of the material in coming to know and experience God as both Creator and Redeemer is anti-sacramental and thus a decidedly deficient theology. The biblical testimony, however, moves consistently in the other direction. God seems not only able and willing, but delighted, to embrace his creation as beloved for its own sake (the work of his hands) and for its capacity to mediate his presence to his creatures.

It's the difference, in the final analysis, between a gospel, that is, a God, a faith, and a church, that makes one free for history and the world and one which makes one flee from history and the world. Or, it's the difference between Christian faith and Gnosticism!

Gnosticism[22] is a dualistic way of thinking that believes that we must seek some kind of secret or special knowledge to enable that bit of the divine or spirit in all of us to escape the dark, fleeting, decaying world of matter and history and flee to the eternal and unchanging world of spirit and light from which it came. Ever

---

22 Most likely arose as a full-blown system in the mid to late 2nd century A.D. as a response to and corruption of Christianity. Various strains of what become Gnosticism were present earlier and addressed in some New Testament documents (e.g. 1 John).

popular, Gnosticism, in different guises, is the Christian faith's most persistent competitor and recurrent temptation through the ages.[23]

So persistent has this Gnostic temptation been that Harold Bloom, in his well-known book *The American Religion*, claims that what we call our religion is in reality a species of Gnosticism! While I believe Bloom overstates his case, he is not fundamentally wrong. There is clearly a tendency to lean in the direction of Gnosticism in interpreting our faith. Consider Bloom's summary statement:

> The American finds God in herself or himself only after finding the freedom to know God by experiencing a total inward solitude. In this solitary freedom, the American is liberated both from other selves and from the created world. He comes to recognize that his spirit is itself uncreated. Knowing that he is the equal of God, the American Religionist can then achieve his true desideratum, mystical communion with his friend, the godhead.[24]

Consider as well the pervasive belief in the immortality of the soul. This belief holds that the soul (the "spiritual" part of us) alone survives death and lives on forever with or in God with whom it shares immortality. This is a Gnostic kind of belief, not Christian. It is based on dualism. The immaterial ("spiritual") part of us, the part that is truly important and "real," survives the demise of the inferior (or even evil) material reality (our bodies) and returns to its source and true home in the "spiritual" realm (God). Much Christian thought about death, life after death, and eternal life are lightly "Christianized" versions of this belief.

God is indeed "spirit" and we must worship him "in spirit and in truth" (John 4:24). Yet God's own love for us moved him to become flesh and live among us in and as Jesus of Nazareth so we could see and touch, and taste and smell God's own gracious and

---

23   See Philip Jenkins, "The Heresy that Wouldn't Die," *Christian History & Biography* 96 (Fall 2007), and most recently in Dan Brown's bestseller The DaVinci Code.

24   Harold Bloom, *The American Religion: The Emergence of the Post-Christian Nation* (New York: Simon & Schuster, 1992), 189.

truthful glory. Jesus Christ, then, is God's chief sacrament (Karl Barth).[25] He is the incontestable evidence that creation not only can but in fact does mediate God's presence! Spirit and flesh are not opposites to be played off against one another. They are part and parcel of the one reality in which God has given us to live. Indeed, the whole material creation is in truth what John Calvin called the "theater of God's glory."[26]

Let's look at some other examples of the way dualism "shrinks" the biblical gospel and robs us not only of its truth but of the fullness of life and experience promised to us in that very gospel!

Christ

Firstly, and most importantly, this dualistic, anti-sacramental gospel shrinks our view of Christ. Consider these questions:

What is the ultimate importance of Christ's becoming human if humanity is on the way to becoming "spiritual" (that is, bodiless, immaterial)?[27]

How about his remaining human, forever? Christ's "bodily" resurrection and ascension into heaven mean just that. Henceforth, the second person of the trinity retains his body. He lives and reigns forever as Jesus Christ, the Word made flesh! Is Jesus' body the only bit of the first creation that makes it into "heaven"? That seems very odd!

What about Jesus as God's agent of creation (Colossians 1:15-20)? Was his work defective even though his Father pronounced it "very good" (Genesis 1:31)? Or is there to be no justice for the creation itself for the degradations and horrors imposed on it by humanity through the millennia, even though God covenanted himself to its care and protection both before and after the Flood (Genesis 9:1-17; see also Romans 8:19-21)? What "good news"

---

25 Editor's introduction to Karl Barth, *Church Dogmatics* 4.4: "Strictly speaking, Barth holds, there is only one sacrament, Jesus Christ Himself, for only in the incarnation of the Son of God in the man Jesus is there a real sacramental unity between God and man."

26 John Calvin, *Institutes of the Christian Religion*, 1.5.1.

27 Or, why does Christmas matter?

does this gospel bring to an age haunted with guilty fears and nightmares of ecological devastation? How is creation related to salvation?

In what way can this Jesus be called a "Savior"? Salvation in the Bible means rescue and restoration from all that destroys, demeans, and diminishes life. In fact, the same Greek word, sōzō, means both to "save" and to "heal." A "Savior," then, restores fullness of life to those from whom death has taken it. A disembodied, immaterial existence in heaven is after all how we tend to define death itself! If there is no restoration to the embodied existence God intended, there is no salvation. Unless salvation is redefined, if Jesus only "saves" some inner part of us (usually called "soul" or "spirit") for eternity, then he hasn't saved us at all!

What "good news" does such a gospel bring to us, whose life spans comprise the growth, decline, and finally, death of our bodies? Are we simply to "shuffle off this mortal coil" (Hamlet) without further ado or should we expect (as per God's promises) that life in his New Creation will be more and not less than life in this world? Are we to never experience life in our bodies as the Creator intended it? And will God's own purpose for life on this planet (Genesis 1 and 2) be forever frustrated as well?

Worship

Our traditional version of the gospel also "shrinks" worship by marginalizing the roles of the sacraments, particularly baptism and the Lord's Supper. This is true even in many more liturgical churches. To the degree that these central gifts of God given to energize and sustain us in an ever-deepening relationship to him and his work in the world seem largely unintelligible, dispensable, peripheral, and powerless, this testifies to our ongoing discomfort with or disbelief in God's involvement with and concern for the physical and material, or in other words, dualism.

We are left with worship that centers on the pulpit and the preached Word instead of the ancient historical pattern of worship which had double foci in preaching and the Lord's Supper. Our belief in the sufficiency of preaching alone is rooted not simply in the Reformation emphasis on "Scripture Alone" but is reinforced by dualism's preference for the inward and Gnosticism's insistence on "knowledge" as the key to unlocking the spiritual journey.

Faith

Next we turn to faith, the way we relate to God. Everything "spiritual" (i.e. important) happens in our soul/spirit/heart. Faith is privatized and individualized; it is what happens between us and God in our inner lives. In faith we accept God's forgiveness through Jesus in our hearts and are thereby assured of our salvation. Our chief task through the remainder of life, if we are conservative, is to keep our inner life with God strong and healthy. That usually takes the form of a regular devotional life and developing a sound grasp of the essential truths of Christianity. If we are more liberal, the task is to allow our faith to motivate us to fulfill the ideals of loving God and neighbor. In either case faith is one's own individual affair, drawing one deeper inward into oneself, wherein we find the impetus and resource for living a "Christian" life.

In truth, and I will spell this out in more detail throughout this book, the reality of faith according to the Bible is communal. Faith incorporates us, body and spirit, into Christ and relates us to his people (Ephesians 2:1-10). Faith only grows in the rich soil of the community's culture – its worship, life together, discipline, and Spirit-given gifts (1 Corinthians 12). And finally, faith's most powerful witness to the world is a corporate body living a pattern of distinctive and countercultural life in the world!

Church

If faith is inward, individual, private and focused on ideas and ideals, there is no necessary connection to or reason for the church. It becomes what has been called "a voluntary association of like-minded people who are free to join or leave based on their private agreement or disagreement with that association's agenda."[28]

Inevitably, this mind-set locks the church into a consumer mode. The church's staff assume the role of vendors of religious goods and services, while members who consume such goods and services ceaselessly demanding more and better as a condition of their continued participation. If this resonates with your experience of church, it should! This is the prevailing model of church in North America and another specimen of the incredible shrinking gospel that afflicts us all.

The Bible again offers a different view. While in no way denying or diminishing the need for each person to respond to God's call and claim on their lives, the covenant community of God's people is the indispensable context in which such faith is evoked, nurtured, equipped, and sent into the world to serve. There are no "Lone Ranger" disciples.

Indeed, scripture knows nothing of "a voluntary association of like-minded people"! It only knows a God who chooses and calls people into commitment to him in ongoing and accountable relationship to the other members so called and claimed by God for the sake of the world. Paul calls us the "body" of Christ (1 Corinthians 12) to make clear how inextricably and organically related members of one another we are (see also Romans 12:5-6). We will return to this theme time and again in this study.

The "Gospel" of the Defeat of God

The most disastrous effect of this "Incredible Shrinking Gospel," however, is that it unwittingly promotes a "gospel" of a defeated God. Here's how this plays out. God created this world as our eternal habitation on which to share with him as the embodied creatures he made us. If after sin, all God manages to do is save a part of us (our soul) for an unembodied eternal "spiritual" existence

---

28   See the interesting essay from an Anglican perspective, "Two Rival Versions of Modern Thinking" at Anglicans ALL (www.duomo. ac.nz/?p=991)

with him in heaven after death, his original reasons for creating us and the world have been defeated. To proclaim the salvation of our souls and eternal life after death in heaven is tantamount to declaring that God, despite his best efforts, could not or would not realize his reasons for creating us and the world or had a better idea in midstream and changed his mind.

No one intends this, mind you. Not at all. Those who proclaim this "gospel" want only to glorify God and minister to the world he loves. Ironically, though, the "Incredible Shrinking Gospel" they embrace thwarts their good intentions and keeps them from proclaiming the genuine gospel to the world![29]

In sum, if you buy into any or all of the following, you may have an "Incredible Shrinking Gospel", that is, one infected with dualistic, Gnostic tendencies:

- ✓ salvation is freedom from the world, earth, and body,
- ✓ salvation is realized primarily at the end of life (death, Christ's return), Jesus' deity is more important than his humanity,
- ✓ faith is inward, individual, and focused on ideas and ideals,
- ✓ hope is defined as bodiless, immaterial, life with God in heaven,
- ✓ the church is helpful but not necessary to spiritual growth,
- ✓ the sacraments don't really make much sense to you, and
- ✓ the gospel you proclaim unwittingly announces the defeat of God!

Let's see if we can "unshrink" the gospel back to its original size and shape. Jesus' life and work will be our guide after we look at the key terms "Empire of God" and "Gospel" to prepare the way.

---

29 Lee Wyatt, "The Gospel of the Defeated God," marginalchristianity.blog-spot.com, 6/7/2014.

PART 2: REVISITING JESUS

CHAPTER 3:

EVANGELISM ESSENTIALS: THE EMPIRE OF GOD

*Now after John was arrested, Jesus came to Galilee, pro-
claiming the good news of God, and saying, "The time is
fulfilled, and the Empire of God has come near; repent, and
believe in the good news."*   (Mark 1:14-15)

EMPIRE OF GOD

In the New Testament evangelism swivels around two concepts.
Of these two words, one, "Gospel" is used more frequently than the
other, "Empire of God," though both have become unmoored from
their biblical settings. It is of extraordinary importance to reconnect
those concepts with that setting. Discovering what they "meant"
will help us to see how far contemporary usage of these terms has
strayed from the Bible's use of them and perhaps give us benchmarks against which to measure our understanding of evangelism.

Let's begin with "Empire of God." This phrase is usually
translated "Kingdom of God." However, there are fewer and fewer
monarchies around these days. And many of those that remain
are figureheads whom we don't take seriously as political leaders.
In our world and experience it is "empire" that best captures what
this biblical phrase connotes. "Empire of God" in the Scriptures
means the worldwide, public, political/religious rule of Israel's God.
In New Testament times the Roman Empire held sway over the
known world. Its ruler, or "King," was Caesar, the emperor. His
"Empire" was the Empire. Those terms mean the same thing in
Jesus' announcement of the "Empire of God." Its ruler, or "King,"

or Caesar, was Israel's God. His domain was all of creation. God, like Caesar, intended to rule every dimension of his people's lives. In our own day, with the revival of talk of an American Empire with pretensions to shape the rest of the world in its image and for its benefit, I believe "Empire" is the most appropriate way to translate this phrase.

Scholars of all stripes, who agree on little else, agree that the "Empire of God" is the central message Jesus preached during his earthly ministry.[30] Mark 1:14-15 is characteristic: "Now after John was arrested, Jesus came to Galilee, proclaiming the gospel* of God,* [15]and saying, 'The time is fulfilled, and the Empire of God has come near;* repent, and believe in the gospel.'" The "Empire of God" here comprises the center of the "gospel," which itself means "good news." Thus, "Empire of God" and "gospel" are correlates. The "Empire of God" is what the "gospel," the "good news" from God, is all about.

"Empire of God" is, as I noted above, the longstanding Jewish hope that God would one day establish his rule over all creation and all peoples of the earth. God would return to Jerusalem in victory, having defeated all his foes, brought peace to the earth, and establish his rule in the midst of his people, Israel. Isaiah 52:7-10 gives beautiful voice to this hope:

> *How beautiful upon the mountains are the feet of the messenger who announces peace, who brings good news, who announces salvation, who says to Zion, 'Your God reigns.' [8]Listen! Your sentinels lift up their voices, together they sing for joy; for in plain sight they see the return of the Lord to Zion. [9]Break forth together into singing, you ruins of Jerusalem; for the Lord has comforted his people, he has redeemed Jerusalem. [10]The Lord has bared his holy arm before the eyes of all the nations; and all the ends of the earth shall see the salvation of our God.*

---

30 Though not all agree on what the phrase means.

Here "Empire" occurs in verbal form, "Your God has taken up imperial rule," and is correlated with "salvation" and "peace," and named "good news." Further, this divine rule or salvation, this "Empire" is a public affair, a changed situation on the stage of human history, God's work with all the nations as spectators.

This hope for God's Empire is what Jesus announces in Galilee and it is that hope that leads him to gather followers, organize them under twelve leaders ("apostles") as the reconstituted people of God, Israel. This new Israel is to fulfill the mission that ancient Israel failed to complete – to be the people through whom God would spread his blessings everywhere (Genesis 12:3). It is that hope that animates Jesus to confront the powers within traditional Judaism, the Roman authorities, and even Satan himself. It is that hope that enabled Jesus to embrace even the suffering and death on the cross because of what he believed God was doing and would do that terrible Friday on Golgotha and afterward. And it is that Empire hope that Jesus continued to nurture in his followers after his resurrection (Acts 1:6-8).[31]

This Empire of God idea gains traction when we ask ourselves, "Why was Jesus crucified anyway?" If Jesus' announcement consisted in: God's coming rule (as an inner reality); God the Father and the infinite value of the human soul; and the commandment to love one another (as classically presented by the eminent church historian Adolf Harnack at the beginning of the last century[32]), it is difficult to know why anyone considered him a threat or bothered to crucify him! Think of the hippies in the sixties and seventies, preaching love for all, human brotherhood, and what a wonderful world it would be if everyone would follow that simple creed. They might have annoyed you; you might have resented them living their lifestyle on the backs of all who worked hard to make America prosperous; but you wouldn't have killed them. They weren't a threat to the social order, they were parasitic on it.

---

31 Notice that Jesus rebuffs only the disciples' desire to know the timeline of the Empire's arrival, not their hope for the Empire to come!

32 See www.demo.lutherproductions.com/historytutor/basic/modern/people/harnack.htm

Some of the hippies became threats, though, when they mobilized and formed movements with definite social-political agendas contrary to the prevailing arrangement of American society. Then we took serious notice of them. The government mobilized itself against them, armed confrontations ensued, and people died living for the aims of their movement.

So long as we believe that Jesus teaches a divine rule like that described by Harnack (a "hippie" Empire, we might almost say), and in large measure we do,[33] we cannot find a satisfactory historical explanation of what Jesus did to upset authorities enough for them to crucify him. Jesus' death only makes historical sense if we realize that the empire he announced was a social-political-religious movement[34] akin to the radical movements of the sixties and seventies. The agenda of this divine Empire called for the restructuring of 1st century Jewish society so it might become what it was supposed to be – the center of God's worldwide Empire! It was this subversive quality of Jesus' announcement and enactment of the dawning of God's Empire that provoked his surveillance, arrest, trial, and execution. And it was that kind of Empire movement he called people to join.

Jesus was, in short, mobilizing a faithful remnant of Israel, reconstituting them as the new and true Israel, that people through whom God would deliver his blessings everywhere in his Empire. That meant confrontation:

- ✓ with the current Jewish power structure for rule within Israel;
- ✓ with the Romans by stirring up the revolutionary desire to purify and restore Israel as God's people again;
- ✓ with other reform and revolutionary movements active in 1st century Palestine; and

---

33 The writings of Joel Osteen would be a contemporary analog.
34 There was no separation between the social, political, and religious spheres in Jesus' time; rather they interpenetrated and mutually modified one another.

✓ it entailed the ever-present possibility of displacement, deprivation, and even death for the community that followed Jesus.

In the movie *The Matrix*, the community gathered around Neo, Morpheus, and Trinity, plays an Empire-like role. They have been enabled to see through the illusions of a world running smoothly (the "Matrix"). They discerned the terrible truth that all people are enslaved to the Matrix, their bodies providing the energy to run the massive computer program that generates the pleasant scenario everyone "thinks" they are living. In reality the world has been largely destroyed, rendered unlivable by the greed and excess of the same powers who now operate the Matrix. The little company on the ironically named vehicle "The Nebuchadnezzar"[35] fights these powers to destroy the Matrix, return everyone to reality, and get on with the work of rebuilding life and re-inhabiting the damaged planet earth.

Jesus and his Empire of God community are on a similar campaign to subvert the way things are in the interest of a vision of how life both can and should be in God's world (his Empire).

To the degree that such a description of Jesus' movement sounds strange (if not offensive) to us, to that degree we have lost touch with the Empire hope of the Old and New Testaments and the fundamental message of Jesus himself!

MARKS OF GOD'S EMPIRE

What can we learn about this Empire of God that features so prominently in Jesus' preaching and ministry and elsewhere in the New Testament as well?[36] It bears at least the following five marks:

---

35 Nebuchadnezzar was the divinely called agent of Judah's destruction and exile in the 6th century B.C.!

36 Though Paul uses the actual phrase "Empire of God" infrequently because he is working largely in non-Jewish contexts, he retains its substance as the "stuff" of his message. It is worth noting that John's Revelation bookends Jesus' announcement of the Empire with the heavenly voices announcing: "The Empire of the world has become the Empire of

1. The Empire of God is a public and political reality.

Far from simply engaging our hearts and leading us to a deeper inner life, the Empire of God enlists us for service in his project of world dominion (Revelation 15:4)! The great Dutch reformed theologian and Prime Minister Abraham Kuyper said it memorably: "In the total expanse of human life there is not a single square inch of which the Christ, who alone is sovereign, does not declare, 'That is mine!'"[37]

Politics is about how we relate to one another and provide access to goods and services as a community. Politics includes the way:

- ✓ power is held and exercised,
- ✓ goods and services delivered and their potential recipients prioritized,
- ✓ justice is administered,
- ✓ status and privilege conferred,
- ✓ honor and shame distributed,
- ✓ values are promoted and passed on, and
- ✓ enemies envisioned and engaged.

The Empire of God, too, has its politics, the way its members are to order and live life in the world. Jesus' Sermon on the Mount (Matthew 5-7)[38] is one key example. And it is worth noting that in the Bible the fundamental measure of a community's health and well-being, and thus the legitimacy of the way they order and live life together, their politics, is measured by the quality of their care for the poor and needy (Isaiah 58).

2. The Empire of God is subversive and radical.

Jesus' announcement of the Empire's arrival both deconstructs the way things are (subversive) and opens the possibility for re-

---

our Lord and of his Messiah, and he will rule forever and ever" (Revelation 11:15)!

37 Quote from Kuyper's inaugural address at the dedication of the Free University in Amsterdam, The Netherlands.

38 More on the Sermon on the Mount in Chapter 7.

construction from the ground up (radical). His parables are chief examples. Take the collection of parables in Matthew 13 on the nature of God's Empire. Each of these parables subverts normal expectations of and assumptions about the character, spread, and speed of growth of the propagation and discovery of God's Empire. Under God's rule "business as usual" no longer applies. As we enter God's Empire we discover that "we're not in Kansas anymore"! In short, we discover that we're not where we thought we were with regard to doing God's work and that things work very differently when God's in charge.

In deconstructing a set of assumptions that no longer apply, these parables also take us to the root (radix, Latin root of radical) where we can begin again, listening to and looking for God's ways with open minds and hearts. There's a whole new set of assumptions and practices we must learn and internalize to work effectively and faithfully in it. The parables open this new world, this imperial rule of God, up to us that we may enter and begin to learn our way around in it and get familiar with its politics.

Subverting and radicalizing, however, do have a cost. They entail misunderstanding, hostile scrutiny, and even conflict. Following Jesus, then, requires that we count the cost of such allegiance.

3. The Empire of God is personal and cosmic.

The call and lure of God's Empire is as personal as the little children Jesus welcomed into his presence (Matthew 19:13-15) and as intimate as the Father numbering the hairs on our heads (Matthew 10:30); as cosmic as Jesus' declaration that "all authority in heaven and on earth" has been given to him, the farthest reaches of God's creative work (Colossians 1:20) and as deep as the furthest hell (1 Peter 3:19ff.). The relational (personal) and structural (cosmic) go together as we see Paul integrate them in Romans 8:19ff. and Ephesians 1. Either without the other tears asunder what God has put together!

New Testament scholar Scot McKnight reflects on this mark of the Empire in terms of the "little gospel" and the "robust gospel":

> "The little gospel promises me personal salvation and eternal life. But the robust gospel doesn't stop there. It also promises a new society and a new creation. When Jesus stood up to read Isaiah 61 in the synagogue at Nazareth, then sat down and declared that this prophetic vision was now coming to pass through him, there was more than personal redemption at work. God's Empire, the society where God's will is established and lived, was now officially at work in his followers. That society was overturning the injustices and exclusions of the empire and establishing an inclusive and just alternative".[39]

4. The Empire of God is gift and task.

In the gospels the primary activity of humans in relation to God's Empire is to "receive" or "enter" it. We do not "build" the Empire, nor do we "plan" it; nor do we "bring it in." Rather, we encounter God's Empire as a gracious gift in the gospel. We "enter" it or not when we encounter it. It is a gift to embrace or hold at arm's length, but always a gift.

Though we do not "build" or "plan" or "bring in" God's Empire, we are called to "enter" it. This means becoming a part of God's imperial work, a member of Jesus' Empire community. And that means we have tasks to do, work appropriate to the Empire to which we have been called. We do this work, these tasks, not to enter this Empire but because we have already been graciously welcomed into it by God's grace and goodness.

This gift and this task can never be separated because they are part and parcel of a relationship and relationships have ties and obligations intrinsic to them. Yet, even though they cannot be separated, we must keep them ordered as we just observed – God's initiative always precedes and evokes our response. Our work, as

---

39   Scot McKnight, "The 8 Marks of a Robust Gospel" at www.christianity-today.com/ct/2008/march/13.36html

response to God's gift of his Empire, must flow out of the relationship between God and us created by his gift. Thus, God's command is never to be heard without his promise and gift preceding (even if the promise and gift remain implicit). Nor is his gift to be presumed upon and used for our own purposes as if we are not implicated by our entering God's Empire to now do God's bidding, God's way!

In all of this a key truth emerges: the good news (or gospel) of God's Empire is more about who we are called to be and will by God's grace be than about who we have been and how we have failed![40]

5. God's Empire is both present and future.

The Empire is here with Jesus' appearance on the scene; yet it is not fully here till he returns. It has dawned but is not yet at noonday high. It has been inaugurated.[41] As an inauguration ceremony only begins a presidency whose full significance and impact will not be seen for years to come, so Jesus' earthly ministry capped by death, resurrection, and ascension decisively and finally inaugurates the presence and reality of God's Empire. The full triumph and unopposed establishment of that Empire will not, however, occur till Jesus' returns.

As those who "enter" God's Empire, we live within the tension of its "already-not yet" character. Allied troops in World War II experienced D-Day in Normandy as the turning point in the struggle in the European theater. After Normandy the outcome there was no longer in doubt. However, it was nearly a year till V-Day, the actual end of the fighting. Allied troops, though victorious, had to remain alert and battle-ready with skills practiced and finely honed. They had to fight on in the "mop-up" battles that rooted out the remaining pockets of Axis resistance to the inevitability of Allied victory. Only with V-Day, nearly a year later, were they able to relax

---

40   More on this in Chapter 13: And So ...
41   I use the language of "inaugurated" because New Testament scholars often speak of this view of the "Empire present-yet-future" as "inaugurated eschatology."

and enjoy the fruits of victory. This is a wonderful analogy for God's Empire and for our role in it. D-Day occurred on that first Easter weekend when Jesus rose from the grave. V-Day, however, is yet to happen. Thus we, like those Allied forces, must remain alert, fully armored with God's own gear (Ephesians 6:10-20) for the struggle ahead as we work to implement Christ's victory in the world.

This Empire is what Jesus is all about. The appearance of God's rule in Jesus is the content of the gospel. It is the good news He announced. To summarize, God's Empire is:

- ✓ a public and political reality,
- ✓ subversive and radical,
- ✓ personal and cosmic
- ✓ gift and task
- ✓ present and future

The preaching and living out of the gospel by communities of Jesus' followers is the form of the Empire's furtherance in the world. Why did Jesus use this language of "gospel" and how does it relate to his "Empire" language? That the subject of our next chapter.

CHAPTER 4

EVANGELISM ESSENTIALS: GOSPEL

Now after John was arrested, Jesus came to Galilee, proclaiming the good news of God, and saying, "The time is fulfilled, and the Empire of God has come near;* repent, and believe in the good news." (Mark 1:14-15)

GOSPEL

Surprisingly, "gospel" (the "evangel" of evangelism!) is a secular word! There is nothing religious about it. It belongs to the imperial lexicon of the Roman Empire and refers to acclamations of victory or announcements of the birth of an heir to the emperor. Messengers fanned out from Rome across the empire bearing such tidings of great joy, the good news, the gospel, concerning matters like the above.

Isaiah 52:7-10, which we looked at earlier, is a paradigm case for understanding what a "gospel" is:

How beautiful upon the mountains are the feet of the messenger who announces peace, who brings good news, who announces salvation, who says to Zion, 'Your God reigns.' Listen! Your sentinels lift up their voices, together they sing for joy; for in plain sight they see the return of the Lord to Zion. Break forth together into singing, you ruins of Jerusalem; for the Lord has comforted his people, he has redeemed Jerusalem. The Lord has bared his holy arm before the eyes of all the nations; and all the ends of the earth shall see the salvation of our God.

From this passage it is clear that "good news" (gospel) is public (from the mountain tops, v.7; and "all the nations," v.10), its content is "salvation" (the rescue of the people from exile; v.7), which means the "Empire" of Israel's God (v.8). Thus announcing the gospel means declaring God's work as a matter of public concern, an announcement of the advent (which is also a "return," v.8) of another actor on the world scene, a power whose presence and activity changes the way the world is ordered and works as well as the lives of every person in it.

Jesus commandeers this secular, imperial language for his own announcement of God's Empire. The church too appropriates this political language by titling its accounts of Jesus "Gospels." He announced God's Empire. His followers acclaimed him as Lord (*kurios* - another term the emperors arrogated to themselves). To 1st century eyes and ears, these terms were unmistakably political manifestos challenging both the legitimacy and longevity of those then sitting in seats and halls of power.

As leader of this new movement, acting with an unprecedented authority and performing mighty acts of power, Jesus could (in his opponent's eyes) be none other than a "wannabe" "king." When he gathered followers and called them "church" (Matthew 16:18; 18:15,17), another secular, political word (*ekklesia* -"town assembly"), he again signaled the public and political nature of his people. By entrusting to them both his authority and message (Matthew 10), Jesus in effect made them his political agents. He also made them liable as was he to the wrath of the powers that be. No wonder Jesus turned away would-be followers who pleaded more urgent responsibilities as reasons for delaying their discipleship (Luke 9:57-62). This work was too important and the consequences too profound for any but those willing to totally commit themselves!

The old saying, "If it looks like a duck, walks like a duck, and quacks like a duck, then it's probably a duck," applies here. Jesus' contemporaries had experienced enough would-be Messiahs doing just what Jesus appeared to be doing not to conclude that he was but another one of them. Like them he announced the arrival of

God's Empire to set all things right and claimed to reestablish Israel and her symbols, Sabbath, Torah (Law), and Temple, as preeminent in the world and to forever be the place of God's presence and rule. The genius of Jesus was that he was coy and subtle enough to allow such impressions to gather all the while subverting and redefining them at every turn. No wonder he told his hearers, disciple and onlooker alike, "Let anyone with ears listen!

So, "Empire" and "gospel" turn out to be companion terms borrowed from imperial vocabulary to position Jesus' movement as a genuine flesh and blood movement of opposition to the Roman empire and other forms of Judaism (Pharisees, Sadducees, Essenes, Zealots) of that time. True, Jesus said his Empire was not of this world (John 18:36). But this does not mean it is "otherworldly" (that is, spiritual, immaterial, an inner reality).[42] Rather, this is John's characteristic way of identifying the source of something. Jesus' Empire, then, does not derive from this world; its origin, assumptions, directions, tactics, and goal all come from God. This is why Jesus tells Pilate that because his Empire is not of this world, his disciples will not resort to violence on his and its behalf. Other resources are available to this movement and its countercultural way of life. Though God's Empire is more than simply another claimant to rule and authority, far, far more, it is not less, never less, than a community of people living out God's rule in a distinctive way of life that challenge the norms and values of the status quo. This community and its distinctive way of life bears witness to all peoples and to the creation itself of the good news that God's rule is for the abundant flourishing of his creatures and the entire cosmos under his loving provision and protection.[43]

---

42 Another expression of dualism at work.

43 Even though our focus is primarily on Jesus, the situation is no different with Paul. N. T. Wright writes: "It is not difficult to see how this "gospel" functions for Paul. Theologically, it belongs completely with Isaiah's ringing monotheistic affirmations that YHWH and YHWH alone is the true god, the only creator, the only soveEmpire of the world, and that the gods of the nations are contemptible idols whose devotees are deceived, at best wasting their time and at worst under the sway of demons. Politically, it cannot but have been heard as a summons to allegiance to "another

Now that's a gospel our world needs to see and hear and a Empire it needs to experience! Thanks be to God that it is this gospel of the Empire of God we are called to and privileged to work for and share for Jesus' sake!

WHAT THE GOSPEL (AND EVANGELISM) IS NOT

In light of this analysis, we can ask, if the gospel is as I have described it, what can we say about the "shrunken" versions we explored earlier and their proclamation? We can say, in contrast to them, what the gospel and what evangelism is not.

The gospel is not a "plan of personal salvation." Many presentations of the gospel amount to telling others that Jesus came to save them and enable them to go to heaven when they die if they believe this "good news." Billy Graham's preaching, Campus Crusade's "The Four Spiritual Laws," and the Evangelism Explosion program of the Coral Ridge Presbyterian Church in Florida are well-known examples of this way of understanding and presenting the gospel.

The focus here is to help people discover and/or admit that they are troubled sinners in need of help from beyond themselves, and to turn to Jesus and receive his forgiveness and healing.

That many have indeed found forgiveness and new life through Christ through this kind of evangelism cannot (and should not) be gainsaid. Though this too is a "shrunken" version of the gospel, it would be churlish to claim that God has not used this (or any of the other "shrunken" gospels we will look at!) in significant ways. None of our evangelism is perfect. If it needed to be, God would have precious little to work with from us![44]

---

king", which is of course precisely what Luke says Paul was accused of saying (Acts 17:7). Practically, this means that Paul, in announcing the gospel, was more like a royal herald than a religious preacher or theological teacher" ("Paul's Gospel and Caesar's Empire," www.ntwrightpage. com).

44 It is said the D. L. Moody, the great 19th century evangellst, was once criticized for the way he did evangelism. After several minutes of this, Moody asked his critic how he did evangelism. The man snorted, "I do

Still, it must be noted that this individualistic focus and dualistically framed gospel (that is, individual salvation as going to heaven after one dies), is a reduced gospel. In the gospel we are to proclaim, God's work is more expansive, world and cosmos-embracing, and concerned with the quality of life in this world as well as the next, than this kind of evangelism. Though popular and time-honored, this "gospel" too is "shrunken"; it is not the "evangel" we are to announce to the world.

The gospel does indeed entail this "good news" of personal salvation, of individual forgiveness and healing as a corollary to its announcement of what God has done and is doing for humankind and the world. However, personal salvation is not what the gospel is "about." That is, God's "plan" is not about the salvation of individuals. Rather, as we have seen, God aims at something much larger than that, nothing less than the redemption, reconciliation, and recreation of the entire cosmos around Jesus Christ (Ephesians 1:10; Colossians 1:15-20). Evangelism, then, is not primarily about saving individual "souls" for heaven. Rather, we announce the full scope of God's design and issue a call for all to join in!

The gospel is also not a political agenda to reform or revolutionize society in the interests of peace and justice. Indeed, the church's primary political responsibility is to be the church. In its existence and life as God's people, the church is to demonstrate to the world that new quality of life, God's shalom, in all it says and does. The church should offer a contrast to the distorted values and priorities that rule society outside and around it. The church should not reflect a religious version of the forms of injustice and oppression that plague the larger communities in which it lives.

Evangelism is the announcement that in and through Jesus of Nazareth such a people now exist among the peoples of the world. The gospel calls such a people into being and depends upon their presence for its credibility! Being that people, that polis[45] (or City

---

not do evangelism, sir!" "Then I like the way I do it wrong better than the way you don't do it all," Moody replied.

45 Polis is Latin for "city" and the root of our word "political."

of God as St, Augustine put it) is our primary task. Our politics is demonstrating to the world in daily life the reality of God's Empire we have received as a gift from God.

That does not mean, of course, that we do not also seek the "welfare of the city" (Jeremiah 29:4-9). Though not "of" the world, we are most definitely "in" the world. To share God's "righteousness," that is, his passion to set all things right, impels us to reach out to our neighbors and work with them to advance and enhance the peace and justice of the larger community. Because the convictions and priorities that drive us are those of God's Empire, we will not participate in a doctrinaire political fashion. That is, we will not identify God's Empire with a particular political party's platform[46] or function as a party loyalist. Our politics in the larger community will be eclectic, unpredictable, and consistent only with the agenda of God's Empire.

The gospel is not "getting religion." God is not offering the world the chance to discover a new dimension of life, called "religion," that enhances, or rounds out, or offers resources for living the rest of life more effectively, productively, happily. This appears to be the gospel that Joel Osteen preaches. His books *Become a Better You: 7 Keys to Improving Your Life Every Day* and *Your Best Life Now: 7 Steps to Living at Your Full Potential* bear eloquent witness to this.

The gospel is about all of life. The secular-sacred division that seems second nature to us was completely foreign to life in the ancient world and varied contexts from which the Bible arose. What we call "religion" and life were co-extensive. Things having to do with deity directly impinged on the things of everyday life. That dealings with the deity might be confined to a "religious" dimension or sector of life was simply unthinkable to them. Biblical thought rejects any such separation. It demands that the totality of our lives conform to God's design rather than God's resources supporting and enhancing our own design for our lives. After all, it

---

46 The "God is Not a Republican or a Democrat" movement in the 2008 elections sounds the right note!

is *Our Utmost for His Highest*[47] not *His Utmost for My Highest*. That means evangelism is not about embracing religion or becoming a religious person! It is about committing ourselves and our resources to God's subversive and radical Empire of peace and justice led by the risen Jesus himself.

Nor is the gospel a religious experience. In an age which thirsts for and lives on experiences,[48] temptations to reinterpret the gospel as a form of religious or spiritual experience abound. Efforts to respond to the current quests for spirituality permeating our culture too often aim for relevance dictated by what we believe are people's "felt needs" and modes of presentation that will "move" them. So we build auditoriums with little or no Christian imagery or symbolism as sanctuaries, practice "entertainment" evangelism,[49] deliver self-help nostrums with a thin veneer of religion,[50] and aim at helping people to adjust to the stresses and strains of living and "feel good" about their life in the world.[51]

This gospel is a gospel of religious experience transformed into a commodity to be consumed by customers searching for the best religious goods and services at the best price. Programs and activities galore are designed and marketed (often expertly) to attract and retain the desired target audience(s).[52] This gospel, however, no matter how well presented, has not and will not result in the disciple-making Jesus commissioned and empowered his people to do (Matthew 28:19).[53] Evangelism with this sort of consumer-gospel

---

47 Oswald Chambers, *My Utmost for His Highest*, (Discovery House Publishers, 2008).

48 More on this in Chapter 12: Wither Evangelism?

49 Walt Kallestad, *Entertainment Evangelism: Taking the Church Public* (Nashville: Abingdon Press, 1996).

50 In addition to Joel Osteen, Robert Schuller is a parade example of this.

51 Paul Louis Metzger, *Consuming Jesus: Beyond Race and Class Divisions in a Consumer Church* (Grand Rapids: Wm. B. Eerdmans Publishing Co., 2007), 5-6.

52 The main difference in this regard between conservative and mainline churches is that the former are much better at it than the latter!

53 The recent courageous disclosure of this reality by Willow Church Church, the biggest and perhaps the best practitioner of this kind of ministry, is a striking case in point.

is most definitely not that practiced and authorized by the New Testament! According to Jesus, the call to enter God's Empire is fraught with uncertainties and inconveniences. Did he not warn would-be disciples of the cost of commitment to God's Empire (Matthew 8:18-22)?

Finally, the gospel is not about going to church and joining a religious institution. In most mainline churches evangelism is reduced to inviting others to visit our church. Such invitations are a more active form of hospitality and welcome than we are used to extending to others, and is certainly a good thing to do, but to call it evangelism is to stretch the meaning of the word beyond recognizable shape. Announcing the good news has a far more compelling content than this!

EMPIRE AND GOSPEL: SUMMARY

The Empire of God and the gospel are companion terms in the biblical lexicon. In Chapter 3 we discovered that God's Empire

is a reality that is:
public and political
subversive and radical
personal and cosmic
gift and task
present and future

In this chapter we have seen that the gospel we have been entrusted with to share with God's world is one that tenaciously struggles to hold on to the "and" in the characteristics listed above. Lose that "and" in any or all of them and the gospel shrinks right before our eyes. And our participation in the ongoing work of God's Empire is constricted and short-circuited.

Finally, we took these findings and described evangelism in terms of what it is not, that is, in terms of some of the most prevalent distortions we encounter in North American culture. The gospel, and therefore the announcement of that gospel, or evangelism, is not about:

> a plan of personal salvation
> a political reform or revolutionary agenda
> getting religion
> a religious experience
> going to church

Rather the gospel is, as Paul memorably puts it in Romans 1:16-17: "the power of God for salvation to everyone who has faith, to the Jew first and also to the Greek. For in it the righteousness of God is revealed through faith and for faith." The "righteousness of God," God's passion and power to set all things right, that's what the gospel is!

Evangelism as the announcement and demonstration of this divine passion for setting all things right can be nothing other and nothing less than Jesus Christ as the focal point, summation, and goal of God's work of creation and re-creation (Ephesians 1:10). Evangelical proclamation sounds this great note and the gracious and glorious invitation each of us has, unworthy though we all are, to once again, in Christ, take up the responsibilities and response-ability given in him, and live and love in God's shalom as we were meant to from the beginning. Anything less is neither evangelical nor proclamation; anything less is moralistic or psychological advice masquerading as good news. A friend of mine in the straits of a severe struggle in his faith, once desperately cried out, "I need good news, not good advice!" We need, our world needs, desperately needs, good news about something that has been done for us, accomplishing what we cannot and will not do for ourselves. Jesus Christ names such good news; he is such good news; he will always be such good news for God's world!

The ground is now cleared and key terms clarified. It is time to turn to Jesus and fill out in more detail what he teaches us about God's Empire and imperial work in the world and how we are called to participate in it!

CHAPTER 5

THE JESUS READ: THE LORE
OF THE GOSPEL

"'The Spirit of the Lord is upon me,
because he has anointed me to bring good news to the poor.
He has sent me to proclaim release to the captives
and recovery of sight to the blind,
to let the oppressed go free,
¹⁹to proclaim the year of the Lord's favor.'"
²⁰And he rolled up the scroll, gave it back to the at-
tendant, and sat down. The eyes of all in the synagogue
were fixed on him. ²¹Then he began to say to them, "To-
day this scripture has been fulfilled in your hearing."
(Luke 4:18-21)

THE IMPORTANCE OF STORIES

Have you ever wondered why we are such avid storytellers? Why we gravitate to stories to help us understand who we are, our world, and to negotiate difficult passages of life? What are we as people, families, nations, countries, and a world but people linked to or separated from each other by stories? Indeed, it is not too much to say that by our stories you will know us!

Jesus, of course, grew up on Israel's stories, primarily its scriptures.[54] He learned his Father's dream and plan for creation in their pages. He drew his identity and sense of place in the world from these sacred texts. They fed his mind and nourished his heart. He communed with his Father through them. A precocious child

---

54 The Christian Old Testament.

(Luke 2:46-47), his understanding and grasp of Israel's story grew and deepened as his own mission pressed on him. It was this story that framed Jesus' vision and gave him the direction and images by which he fashioned his unique sense of vocation and Messiahship. To that story, *The Jesus Read: Lore of the Gospel* we now turn.

GOD'S DREAM: THE STORY OF CREATION

In the beginning God had a dream. That dream is enshrined in the first two chapters of the Torah,[55] which constitute Act 1 ("Creation") of the biblical story. There Jesus was wooed by the beauty and breadth of God's dream. Imagine it, the first of the two creation stories in Genesis 1-2 sang to him of a world brimming over with lovely and diverse abundance, luxurious and verdant, extravagant beyond measure, wild and free, vitality oozing out of every nook and cranny! Yet also a world so finely tuned and calibrated, so perfectly reflective of its Creator's beauty and perfection that it takes his breath away! This world, so gorgeous and alive, inhabited by a mind-boggling number of creatures and species, air-creatures, land-creatures, water-creatures and more, and all under the oversight and protection of Adam (Hebrew – humanity). Humanity, in its two forms, male and female, reflects and bears God's rule and God's authority over and for this wondrous globe, their delight and duty, as well as their destiny.

And yet again, the second creation story sang Jesus a somewhat different song to a somewhat different end. Now at the center rather than the apex of creation God placed Adam (the human creature) in a garden to "till and keep" it. Now a priest as much as royal representative[56] in the temple that is Eden,[57] Jesus learns

---

55 The first five books of the Old Testament, Genesis to Deuteronomy; also called the Pentateuch.

56 The Hebrew words translated "till" and "keep," when used together in the Old Testament "refer either to Israelites 'serving' God and 'guarding[keeping]' God's word . . . or to priests who 'keep' the 'service' . . . of the Tabernacle." (Beale, *The Temple*, 67).

57 G. J. Wenham, "Sanctuary Symbolism in the Garden of Eden Story," in R. S. Hess and D. T. Tsumara (eds.), *I Studied Inscriptions from Before the Flood* (Winona Lake, IN: Eisenbrauns).

that this priesthood is to be shared. Indeed God says "It is not good that Adam should be alone."[58] And the Creator gives Adam a "helper"[59] (an equal companion) to share in this human privilege and responsibility. She was created not from the man's head to rule over him, nor from his feet to be subordinate to him, but from his side to walk together with him in tilling and keeping the Garden entrusted to their care.

But there is more, the song continues. Look outside of Eden, it invites Jesus. Behold the rest of the world. A river from the garden waters the whole of the surrounding environs (that is, the rest of the world). The divine image-bearers are to extend God's rule and authority out from Eden till it finally embraces the whole world. Until, that is, the whole creation comes to be a sanctuary in which to worship God and serve others![60]

From the intimacy of marriage to the vision of a world embraced in the love and service of the Creator, this second creation song complements the first, filling in some details about the human creatures and the setting out some of the specifics of their calling.

GOD'S NIGHTMARE: THE STORY OF THE FALL

Entranced by this divine dream, Jesus is crushed as the second creation song turns to lament when God's dream is dashed by human sin (Genesis 3-11; Act 2, "Catastrophe" of the biblical story)!

Horror-stricken, Jesus listens to the song recount the first couple and their offspring's trashing of the Creator's vision. Now instead of humanity living in full dependence on God and in harmony and interdependence with themselves, each other, and the

---

58 Genesis 2:18.
59 Of its 22 uses in the Old Testament, the Hebrew word *ezer* is used for God 17 times, to denote military strength 3 times in addition to its 2 uses in Genesis 2. See Marva Dawn, *In the Beginning God: Creation, Culture, and the Spiritual Life* (Downers Grove: InterVarsity Press, 2009), 78.
60 See the discussion in Beale, *The Temple*, 81-83; also Genesis 1:28; Isaiah 45:18.

creation itself, God's shalom is shredded and this fourfold harmony devolves into a foul cacophony, mocking the Creator.

This "damned" litany lurches from fratricide to flood to dispersal to Babel.[61] Throughout it all, however, runs a counter-measure, a note that alone offers hope for the creation. In these stories God responds to humanity's sin by mitigating the judgment he himself pronounces against them. Adam and Eve do not die immediately, God gives them skins to cover themselves, Cain receives God's mark of protection, and Noah and his family are saved from the flood. This gracious, divine counter-measure to humanity's evil and deserved punishment epitomizes the Apostle Paul's great claim in Romans 5:20: "where sin increased, grace abounded all the more." This "grace abounding" emerges here as a central motif running through all of scripture!

GOD CALLS A NEW ADAM: THE STORY OF THE PATRIARCHS

Humanity's delight and destiny, as well as creation's flourishing, now forfeited by Adam and Eve, God undertakes to set all things right again. He begins by choosing a new Adam,[62] calling Abram from Haran and unconditionally making a threefold promise to him and his posterity. From Abram (later renamed "Abraham"[63]) and his wife, Sarai (later renamed "Sarah"[64]), both beyond child-bearing age, God promises to get a great nation. God will bless this people and make them a blessing. And through this people God will bless the rest of creation.[65] God's response to and antidote for sin has begun! This is Act 3 ("Covenant") of the biblical story.

---

61 Genesis 4-11.
62 Wright, *The New Testament and the People of God*, 251: "'I will make Adam first,' says Israel's God in the midrash on Genesis, 'and if he goes astray I will send Abraham to sort it all out,'" The midrash reference is Genesis Rabbah 14:6.
63 "Father of nations."
64 Genesis 17:15.
65 Genesis 12:1-3.

The problem bequeathed to the human race by Adam and Eve's defection from God becomes "focused" now, as it were, on this one family and the people to come from them. God's resolution to the problem of sin and the fulfillment of his eternal purpose will be mediated to the rest of humanity by this family. This is one reason why Israel is so important and the Old Testament so vital to Christian faith.[66]

As Jesus hears this promise to Abram and Sarai he realizes he is hearing the very heart beat of God. Here is his Father's agenda clearly laid out. God intends not simply to set right what has gone wrong but to restore and bring to glorious fulfillment his original dream as well. More than "merely" dealing with sin, God is still intent on realizing his dream of having a creation full of people who live under his gracious rule and embody his shalom throughout the ages. And God will do that through Abraham and his people as they live and serve him in the promised land as a prototype of what all creation and every creature is designed for. This is what being "Israel," God's people, is all about - a means for dealing with the problem of sin and a model for what God's creation should look like!

Genesis 12:1-3, then, is Israel's rationale for being. It reveals God's passion and agenda, which passion and agenda drives the biblical story. This threefold promise – God's intention to get a people, bless that people, and use that people to bless everyone else - encompasses and gives meaning to the ongoing life of Abraham's people. As one of Abraham's people, Jesus accepts this mission and mandate as his own.

God's confirms his gracious choice of this family and people as his chosen people[67] by making a covenant with Abraham.[68] This

---

66 This contrasts strangely with the horrors of Christian anti-semitism through the centuries and the almost total neglect of the Old Testament in most branches of the North American Church. I've have heard more times than I care to remember someone saying, "I'm more of a New Testament Christian."
67 Deuteronomy 7:7ff.
68 Genesis 15.

covenant is subsequently reaffirmed to Isaac[69] and Jacob.[70] It stands as the fundamental plank in Israel's self-understanding. Their glory was in being God's elect people. Their blessing, in this calling is a special relationship to God and the promise of land. Their mandate is to be the vehicle of God's blessing of all other peoples (Figure 2). As we will see Israel embraced the glory and clung to the blessing but more often than not forgot, ignored, or did their best to evade the mandate.

FREEDOM FOR GOD: THE STORY OF MOSES, EXODUS, AND SINAI

Jesus continues to listen as his people's story unfolds in a new chapter. Through the vagaries of history and under the providence of God, Abraham's family ends up in Egypt under the sponsorship of Joseph (Jacob's exiled son turned chief administrator of Pharoah's empire) to weather a famine. After Joseph's death, however, a new Pharaoh grew anxious at the Israelites' increasing numbers and began oppressing them with harsh labor. The people cry out to God and God gives them Moses.

Moses emerges as the Israelites' leader and challenges Pharaoh to let his people go in the name of YHWH.[71] After failed negotiations, a series of divine plagues do the trick and the people leave Egypt. Pharaoh changes his mind, however, chases them down, and soon the people are trapped – the sea behind them, Pharaoh's troops in front of them. YHWH, however, delivers his people with a mighty act, opening the sea for his people to cross and then closing it back again on their Egyptian pursuers. After journeying for some time in the desert, Moses and the people arrive at Mt. Sinai.

---

69 Genesis 26:3-5.
70 Genesis 28:13-14.
71 The personal, covenant name of God revealed to Moses at the burning bush (Exodus 3:14). Jews do not pronounce this sacred name but substitute "Lord" whenever it appears in the biblical text. I will use the four consonants without vowels to respect Jewish convictions concerning this word.

There God formally ratifies his relationship with them, establishing a covenant through Moses at the heart of which lie the Ten Words.[72]

These words constitute the people God has graciously chosen and redeemed as his distinctive covenant people among all peoples and nations, a people through whose life together God and God's way will be made known to the world.[73] The Ten Words form the distinctive life of the people around worship (the words or commandments prohibiting idolatry (basic issue), graven images (sin of and against the eyes), false language toward God (sin of and against the tongue), and Sabbath (sin of and against the body). And from this worship of YHWH flows the community life that pleases YHWH and reflects his character abroad (the remaining six Words).

These Ten Words (and all the other laws given to Israel) are not requirements to merit salvation or gain entry into God's people. God has already seen to that by calling Israel and redeeming the people from Egypt. Redemption has been accomplished; the relationship between YHWH and the people secured by his gracious love and mercy (formalized in the Abrahamic Covenant). The Ten Words guide the people in living out the proper response to such great salvation. As is sometimes said today, these commandments are not given for Israel to keep to "get in" to covenant with God, rather they are given to help them "stay in," that is, function effectively and faithfully as God's covenant people. Thus this Mosaic Covenant made at Mt. Sinai is conditional upon obedience to achieve its purposes of showing forth the life designed by God to the world. However, it is not determinative for salvation, that is, membership in the people of God.

But what kind of world does God desire? What shape is human life to take? How are the Israelites to model this distinctive calling they have received to be the prototype of what YHWH intends for everyone?

---

72 Traditionally called the Ten Commandments though the Hebrew text of Exodus simply calls them the "ten words."

73 Deuteronomy 4:5-8.

Hidden away in the book of Leviticus (and I say "hidden away" because so few people ever read Leviticus anymore), Jesus listens to a stunning and provocative display of the fundamental dynamics of the model Israel was to be for the world. So stunning and provocative, in fact, that Israel itself never quite managed to live it out. So powerfully did this Levitical vision mark Jesus that he picks up the substance and symbolism of this divine dream as the banner under which he marches as he announces and inaugurates the Empire of God. This model is known as the "Jubilee" laws and they are found in Leviticus 25.

In essence, these laws required Israel as a society to build into its pattern of life legal mechanisms that, when practiced, would display YHWH's compassionate justice as the only viable means to genuine human flourishing. These laws promote justice because they show right relationships functioning at every level of society. They are compassionate because they weave a network of these right relationships in which the well-being of the community is fostered only when everyone cares for the well-being of each other, especially the well-being of weak, vulnerable, and needy.

The core of these laws requires a fundamental reorientation of Israel once every generation.[74] First, slaves were to be freed. All were to have the chance to produce and contribute as they were gifted and able to the common future of Israel as God's people. Second, all land was to be returned to the family to which it had been given when Joshua and his generation first settled the land. As the basic form of capital in an agrarian economy, land was fundamental to any hope of long term economic viability. As a consequence, every fiftieth year, Israel was to economically empower each family to be productive members of the community. Haves and have nots were not to be a permanent of life in the community God desires. All this is, of course, rooted in the proper worship of YHWH.[75]

---

74 That is, after seven sabbatical years have passed, sabbatical years being every seventh year. Thus every fiftieth year was to be a Jubilee year. Or it could have been the forty-ninth year depending on how one reads the evidence.

75 Leviticus 25:18.

You may well imagine that those who had benefited and grown comfortable throughout those forty-nine years might not be too anxious for such a "leveling." And they would most likely have sufficient political and economic clout to sabotage it. And that apparently is just what happened. We have no evidence that the Jubilee was ever enacted. And we have only to look within our own hearts to know why! Nevertheless, the Jubilee remains "on the books" as God's as yet unfulfilled dream for his people. And Jesus, once captivated by this monumental vision, could not help but cast his own vision as a reinterpretation of its imagery and substance for his "Empire of God" movement.[76]

Rejecting YHWH: The Story of Kingship

The next major benchmark in the story for Jesus to reflect on follows the wilderness wandering and the people's entering and settling of the promised land. The people grow restive with the invisible kingship of YHWH over them and want a human king like all the other nations.[77] YHWH relents and gives them one but takes all the fun out of being king (as it were). By that I mean that Yahweh so defines what kingship in Israel should be that the king would effectively be merely "a brother among brothers," shorn of the usual accoutrements and perks that accompany kingship.[78]

The first king, Saul, proves a failure. His successor, David, however, succeeds despite significant failures and character flaws.[79] He is the "man after (God's) own heart"[80] and becomes the icon of

---

76 In this respect, the Sermon on the Mount (Matthew 5-7) might serve as Jesus' basic reinterpretation of Jubilee.

77 1 Samuel 8-12.

78 "Deuteronomy accepts kingship under conditions (Dt. 17:14-20) which amount to a condemnation both of the Mesopotamian and Canaanite models and of the way the Israelite history actually worked out," John Howard Yoder, The Jewish-Christian Schism Revisited, Michael G. Cartwright and Peter Ochs (eds.) (Grand Rapids: Wm. B. Eerdmans Publishing Co., 2003), 71.

79 See the brief but helpful reflections of David Firth, "David: Reflecting on Kingship" at www.met-uk.org/met/article.php/?cat=general&id=373&PH).

80 1 Samuel 13:14.

Israel's ideal king. It is with David that YHWH concludes a covenant promising him a never-ending line of descendants on Israel's throne.[81] This Davidic Covenant is essentially a reaffirmation or updating of the Abrahamic Covenant.[82] It is the third of the four great covenants God makes with the children of Abraham (with Abraham, with Moses and the people at Mt. Sinai, with David, and the promise of the New Covenant in Jeremiah 31). Like the first of these covenants this one is also unconditional. Together they express God's determination to have, keep, and use Abraham's people as the vehicle for his blessing the rest of the world. The second, the Mosaic Covenant, assumes this divine determination and gifts the people with YHWH's charter of freedom, the Ten Words.[83] These Ten Words sketch the parameters of YHWH's blessing and the faithfulness of Israel's witness. This, in other words, is how Israel will experience both YHWH's blessing and be herself a blessing to everyone else!

David himself profiles the ideal Israelite king, his priorities, passions, and practices, in Psalm 72, a prayer for his own son Solomon):

> *Give the king your justice, O God,*
> *and your righteousness to a king's son.*
> *May he judge your people with righteousness,*
> *and your poor with justice.*
> *May the mountains yield prosperity for the people,*
> *and the hills, in righteousness.*
> *May he defend the cause of the poor of the people,*
> *give deliverance to the needy,*
> *and crush the oppressor. . .*
>
> *For he delivers the needy when they call,*
> *the poor and those who have no helper.*
> *He has pity on the weak and the needy,*

---

81   2 Samuel 7:1-17.
82   Genesis 15 based on Genesis 12:1-3.
83   Exodus 20:1-17.

and saves the lives of the needy.
From oppression and violence he redeems their life;
and precious is their blood in his sight. . .

May his name endure for ever,
his fame continue as long as the sun.
May all nations be blessed in him;*
may they pronounce him happy.

In this psalm David lays out in royal idiom what God had mandated Adam and Eve to be and do in the creation stories. He also explicitly invokes the third of God's threefold promise to Abraham in Genesis 12:3: "May all nations be blessed in him" (v.17). The king as representative of the people is to be the chief exemplar in his royal role of the life God expects of the people as a whole.

Even though human kingship had not been God's design for Israel, God nonetheless reshapes their sinful insistence for a human monarch in the direction of his original intent. Of course, none of the human kings in either the United Monarchy[84] or the Divided Empire[85] lived up to this royal profile in Psalm 72. This highlights in a poignant way Israel's ultimate failure to be part of God's solution to the problem of human sin. Rather, in failing their mandate to be the people through whom God blesses the world, they only compounded the problem.

These persistent royal failures finally led to the idea that this "Psalm 72" king must be a figure specially sent from God bearing unique gifts and blessings to set Israel and, indeed, the whole world right again. This is the figure of the "Messiah" (literally, "anointed one"; "Christ" in Greek). The coming of the Messiah would be an "eschatological" event. That is, it would be part of the "end times," the decisive intervention of God to finally and fully set all things right. Neither the Messiah nor this divine intervention (often called

---

84 The Empires of Saul, David, and Solomon.
85 The Kings of Judah and Israel from the end of Solomon's Empire to Judah's exile in Babylon in 587 B.C.

"the Day of the Lord" in the Old Testament) were of human origin.[86] They were God's doing.

Messianic hope was alive and restlessly vibrant during Jesus' life time.[87] These hopes, though varied, generally held that the Messiah would lead a great and successful revolt against Israel's oppressors (Rome in Jesus' time), exercising God's judgment on them. The Messiah would then assume leadership in Israel, reform it, and reestablish it as chief among nations. He would oversee the rebuilding of the temple so that God might return to his purified people and reside once more there, directing and guiding them into the new age of fulfillment and glory.

But what kind of Messiah? Jesus came to understand that the current models of Messiahship in Israel were inadequate. Popular, though inadequate. That the devil tempts Jesus (Matthew 4:1-13) with three of these ways to be Messiah in his effort to derail him attests to both their inadequacy (since the devil favors them) as well as their popularity (they must have been well-known enough and plausible enough to have appealed to Jesus to some degree).

What were these three models of Messiahship Jesus judged inadequate?

- ✓ socio-economic provison
- ✓ religious sensationalism
- ✓ political dominance

Why did Jesus reject these models? I think we get our answer later in the gospel when James and John come to Jesus requesting the seats of honor and power on either side of him when his work is successfully concluded (Mark 10:35-45). That leads Jesus to the following critique:

> *"You know that among the Gentiles those whom they recognize as their rulers lord it over them, and their great ones*

---

86 Though the Messiah is thought to be a human and not a divine figure, his mandate, mission, and equipping are a divine calling and a divine gifts.

87 See the discussion of Judas of Galilee at http://www.livius.org/men-mh/Messiah/messianic_claimants04.html

are tyrants over them. ⁴³*But it is not so among you; but whoever wishes to become great among you must be your servant,
⁴⁴and whoever wishes to be first among you must be slave of
all.* ⁴⁵*For the Son of Man came not to be served but to serve,
and give his life a ransom for many."*

Jesus' disciples "know" how the power game is played in the
world. They are aware that it entails a "lording it over" one's un-
derlings, "tyrannizing" them, one-upping others, and scrambling
for a better position higher up on the ladder of success.

Jesus, however, will have none of that. Instead he leaves them
with their jaws lying on the ground when he enjoins on them
an unthinkably new and seemingly impossible burden – equating
greatness with servanthood, with slavery, even with giving up one's
life for others. And more than that, Jesus assumes this will have
some kind of "redemptive" effect!

Now we can see, I think, what Jesus found objectionable in
the devil's messianic offers. Each of them is built on the scaffolding
of the world's way of leadership and achievement. Each of them is
ultimately based on the serpent's inciting Adam and Eve to grab at
his offer to be like God.[88] Israel had tried each of them at various
points in their journey with God too – with disastrous results. Now
the devil tries the same gambit with Jesus. But Jesus refuses to bite.

He goes his own way, or better, God's way, in prayerful dependence on his Father and the Spirit he received at baptism.
Pondering the long story of his people's relationship with God in
light of his growing sense of vocation as their Messiah, Jesus finds
unexpected and unexploited precedents in that story out of which
he fashioned and interpreted his call as Israel's Messiah.

Though other more familiar titles are given to Jesus in the
gospels he tends to shy away from them because they all contain expectations associated with the models of Messiahship he rejected in
the wilderness. There were two other, lesser-used, models, however,
that attracted Jesus. One became his favorite and most frequent

---

88 Genesis 3.

self-designation, "Son of Man," from Daniel 7. There the term speaks of a vindicated and victorious figure (a fluid symbol capable of signifying both an individual and the people of God together) receiving "glory and kingship" from the "Ancient of Days." It carries less baggage than other more widely-used titles (like "Messiah") and a certain ambiguity[89] that leaves Jesus free to fill it with his own content and associations.

The core of Jesus' fresh and unexpected view of Messiah comes from the Servant Songs in Isaiah 40-55, particularly the final song in Isaiah 52:13-53:12. There we find the enigmatic figure of the Suffering Servant who dies at God's hand bearing the sins of his people. His death brings healing and salvation to the people and YHWH raises the Servant up in vindication and glory. Jesus doubtless meditated and prayed at length over this image, drawing from it a way of explaining his peculiar and unprecedented sense of vocation – to be a suffering and dying Messiah in order to save his people. No one in Israel had or would contemplate such a figure. Suffering, death, and Messiah just simply did not go together. That was mixing apples and brussels sprouts, so to speak.

Yet Jesus had come to accept just this kind of Messiahship as his calling from God. So he embraced this image of the Suffering Servant and used it frequently to explain key aspects of who he was and what he was doing to his listeners. Its unfamiliarity and unexpectedness gave Jesus ways to talk about the character of his Empire of God movement that maintained its public and political focus on the community but avoided the nationalistic and militaristic associations of the other messianic models.

This is the reading of his heritage and holy book that fueled Jesus' imagination and steeled his courage for the vocation to which his Father had called him. As we read his story in the four gospels, each writer tells it in such a way that it answers the three questions arising from the great promise of Genesis 12:1-3. How does Jesus go about getting a great people for God? How does he bless that people? And how does he use and promise to use them to bless the

---

89 It can be simply a euphemism for "mortal" as often in Ezekiel.

world? Their answers give us the core content of the "gospel" which we are to proclaim to the world!

CHAPTER 6

THE JESUS CREED:[90] THE CORE OF EVANGELISM

One of the scribes came near and heard them disputing with one another, and seeing that he answered them well, he asked him, "Which commandment is the first of all?"

[29]Jesus answered, "The first is, 'Hear, O Israel: the Lord our God, the Lord is one; [30]you shall love the Lord your God with all your heart, and with all your soul, and with all your mind, and with all your strength.' [31]The second is this, 'You shall love your neighbor as yourself.' There is no other commandment greater than these."

(Mark 12:28-31)

THE *SHEMA* – ISRAEL'S CREED

We have seen that Jesus believed himself the "continuation" of, the "answer" to, the "climax" and "fulfillment" for the ongoing story of Israel's covenantal relationship and journey with YHWH. We noted some of the main features of Jesus' take on that story which he accepted as benchmarks and cues for his own vocation. In this and succeeding chapters we will try to spell out in a bit more detail how Jesus shaped his take on Israel's story into a distinctive way of being Messiah; a way that resolved not only Israel's problem with sin and unfaithfulness but the larger human struggle with same realities rooted in the defection of Adam and Eve in the Garden of Eden. Thus Jesus mission, we will discover, is as particular as his

---

90 I am indebted in this chapter to Scot McKnight's *The Jesus Creed: Loving God, Loving Others* (Brewster, MA: The Paraclete Press, 2004).

life as 1ˢᵗ century Galilean peasant and as universal as the "human problem" we wrestle with today in every corner of the globe, "far as the curse is found" as Isaac Watts put it in his great Christmas carol "Joy to the World."

That the life and death of an obscure 1st century Galilean peasant could have such universal reach and efficacy is a scandal to almost everyone else in the world. "How can someone's death and (alleged) resurrection two thousand years ago have any meaning for me today?" is an oft asked question in our time. Yet this "scandal of particularity," as it is called, remains at the heart of the church's gospel because of our conviction that the Christian God is one who always presses for incarnation, that is, intimacy and identification with his human creatures.[91] Such a drive for incarnation entails particularity; God had to become incarnate as some one, at some time, in some place. There's no such thing as a generic human who relates with equal immediacy to each and every other human being. There are only particular human beings, Jews and Gentiles being the primal pairing. That God chose to become incarnate as a Jew is due to his election of love[92] not to anything intrinsic in being a Jew; that God chose to come in the 1st century at the time of Roman rule was, according to Paul, because in the divine plan this was the "fullness of time."[93] Thus, to answer "why" God took the route of becoming one of us, we respond – his passion for intimacy and identification with his creatures. To answer why he became human as a Jew at that time and in that place, we respond – then and there was the right time, was the right time in God's wisdom and for his purposes.

We have Jesus situated in time and place, and in relation to the story that defined his life and vocation. But how did he go about

91 The question at issue here is whether Jesus would have come and taken human flesh (been incarnate) if humanity had not sinned and gone its own way. This is controversial in the history of theology, but I stand with Duns Scotus and others in believing that incarnation was also a part of God's plan and not simply an emergency measure to deal with the problem of sin.

92 Deuteronomy 7:7.

93 Galatians 4:4.

living out his vocation in that time and place. What animated Jesus, drove him to "keep on keeping on" in the face of rejection and resistance? What did Jesus mutter to himself at those seemingly impossible moments to keep the fire burning to see his mission through to the end?

Most of us have some sort of "mantra" we tell ourselves to keep us engaged when life hits a rough patch or at moments of great import. We might call it our creed. Every group has some kind of creed that focuses its vision and energy: the Pledge of Allegiance, the Boy Scout Motto, "When the going gets tough, the tough get going," "Win One for the 'Gipper!'," "Just Do It!," "The One who Dies with the Most Toys Wins!"

Churches also have creeds that serve to identify them, what they commit to do, and why they do it. The Apostles' and Nicene Creeds are statements that every Christian church affirms, whether officially or unofficially. They are definitional of the two great core truths of Christian faith: the mystery of God as triune and the mystery of the incarnation of Christ.

Judaism too had such a creed. It is called *The Shema* and is found in Deuteronomy 6:4-9:[94]

> *Hear, O Israel: The Lord is our God, the Lord alone.[95]*
> *You shall love the Lord your God with all your heart, and with*
> *all your soul, and with all your might. Keep these words that*
> *I am commanding you today in your heart. Recite them to*
> *your children and talk about them when you are at home and*
> *when you are away, when you lie down and when you rise.*
> *Bind them as a sign on your hand, fix them as an emblem on*
> *your forehead, and write them on the doorposts of your house*
> *and on your gates.*

---

94 *Shema* is the first word in Deuteronomy 6:4-5 in Hebrew.
95 There are some alternative translations for this first phrase. The NRSV footnote lists the following: "The Lord our God is one Lord," "The Lord our God, the Lord is one," or "The Lord is our God, the Lord is one." The basic thrust of the verse is unaffected however, though there are different nuances according to the translation one follows.

The Shema had been the heartbeat of Jewish faith long before Jesus came along. Children were taught *The Shema* as their first prayer and recited it morning and evening throughout their lives. Only the direst circumstances justified skipping a recitation of this creed. Regular immersion in this creed had a powerful shaping effect on the Jews, similar to that on Christians who have regularly prayed the Lord's Prayer or the daily office.[96]

How does *The Shema* shape Jewish spirituality? It makes it incorrigibly YHWH-centered. Awareness of YHWH's presence and power decisively impacts formation of priorities, channels passions in faithful directions, and evokes practices consistent with those priorities and energized by those passions. In a world filled with gods and goddesses thought to control various aspects and areas of life, this breath-taking affirmation of the one God's Lordship over every area of life not only set Israel apart from all other peoples but placed then in inevitable tension with them as well. The first of the Ten Words assumes added meaning in this kind of situation. "You shall have no other gods before me." Not only is this a call to rank YHWH higher than any other deity. If you think of it in spatial terms, it means don't have any other deities in my presence ("before" as "in front of"). And since YHWH is everywhere, it is a call to make your life a deity-free zone outside of total commitment to YHWH. Thus there is no option of trying to make life a little easier by adding one's neighbor's deities to YHWH (below him, of course), even if just for social reasons.

Reciting *The Shema* shapes Jewish spirituality in a second way by making it Torah-focused. The Torah,[97] which means more than simply "Law," something more like "teaching" or "instruction" or "direction," contains Israel's foundational narratives (e.g. the Exodus), the faith-defining covenants (Abraham and Moses), the fundamental laws for both personal and social/political/econom-

---

96 A pattern of regular prayers offered throughout the day according to a schedule and lectionary.

97 The first five books of the Old Testament, Genesis – Deuteronomy.

ic life (e.g. the Ten Words,[98] the Covenant Code,[99] the Holiness Code,[100]) and the figures who exemplify (in both positive and negative ways) the struggle for daily faithfulness.

A third mark of *Shema*-shaping in Jewish spirituality is a communal mindset. Over fifty years ago a British Old Testament scholar named H. Wheeler Robinson wrote a seminal book entitled *Corporate Personality in Ancient Israel* establishing that for Israel, as for most ancient peoples, the community was the primal reality to which they belonged and was prior and primary to the individual person. The concept of an individual relationship with God apart from the community was not even thinkable to the Israelites. Even when the idea of individual responsibility for sin and punishment emerged in Israel (see the prophet Ezekiel), this never overrode its fundamental sense of the priority of the people and community.

Even Torah study was not primarily an individual matter. Rabbi Hananiah ben Teradion, in a saying similar to Jesus' saying in Mathew 18:20, asserts: "When two sit together and words of the Law are spoken between them, the *Shekinah* (presence of God) rests between them."[101]

Israel's creed, *The Shema*, then inculcates a profoundly communal faith. This community, its rituals, worship, Torah study, and daily life together formed the matrix in which a vital and viable faith was nurtured, a faith that has enabled the Jews to endure perhaps more than any other people and to do so in faith.

THE *KADDISH* – ISRAEL'S PRAYER

Israel also had a prayer that played a significant role in forming them as YHWH's people. *The Kaddish* ("The Sanctification" as it is called) joined the Shema as central acts within Jewish worship and piety. *The Kaddish* reads:

---

98 Exodus 20:1-17.
99 Exodus 21-23.
100 Leviticus 17-26.
101 Cited in N. T. Wright, *The Challenge of Jesus: Rediscovering Who Jesus Was and Is* (Downers Grove: InterVarsity Press, 1999), 114.

*Magnified and sanctified be His great name in the world
He created according to His will. May He establish His Empire during your life and during your days, and during the
life of all the house of Israel, speedily and in the near future.
And say Amen.*[102]

It is easy to see that the concerns of the Shema and those of the
Kaddish interlock in mutually reinforcing ways. *The Kaddish*, like
The Shema, is YHWH-centered, Torah-focused, and communal.
Immersed in a life anchored by these two central practices, it is
not hard to imagine a life contoured by the delights in and duties
to YHWH!

Jesus is nowhere more firmly rooted in his Jewish faith and heritage than in his embrace of these two spiritual pillars of Judaism.
His embrace of them, however, is a creative one. He takes them up
and reformulates them in light of his own sense of calling of vocation as Israel's Messiah and his awareness that in and through him
that ancient and fervent hope of the people – the coming of God's
Empire – was beginning to happen. Thus he could not simply let
them stand as they were for the time had changed. Calendar time
(Greek - *chronos*) has given way to fulfilled time, time pregnant with
meaning and new life (Greek - *kairos*). The Empire is now arriving,
it is at hand![103] That means everything is seen in a new light and
nothing remains quite the same.

Jesus has a creed and a reinforcing prayer too! We must observe, though, how he has changed them in light of the new age
of the Empire to discover how they might shape our spirituality
as his followers.

---

102 Cited in McKnight, *The Jesus Creed*, 15. If this sounds reminiscent of Je-
    sus' Lord's Prayer, it is!
103 Mark 1:14-15.

THE GREAT COMMANDMENT – JESUS' CREED

> *One of the scribes came near and heard them disputing with one another, and seeing that he answered them well, he asked him, "Which commandment is the first of all?"*
>
> *Jesus answered, "The first is, 'Hear, O Israel: the Lord our God, the Lord is one; you shall love the Lord your God with all your heart, and with all your soul, and with all your mind, and with all your strength.' The second is this, 'You shall love your neighbor as yourself.' There is no other commandment greater than these."* (Mark 12:28-31)

We are on familiar ground as Jesus begins to respond to the scribe's question about the greatest commandment (which is but another way of asking Jesus "What's your creed?"). Jesus starts with the Shema, where any good Jew would start. There's really no other place to begin than with YHWH-centeredness.

One can only marvel at Jesus' nerve here. He does not stop with the YHWH-centered Shema but adds another piece from Leviticus 19:18: "You shall love your neighbor as yourself." (Didn't know Leviticus had something like that in it, did you?) Jesus adds to the Bible – with another part of the Bible! Only one convinced he was Israel's Messiah and YHWH's beloved son could do such a thing on his own authority! Yet the addition of Leviticus 19:18 does not so much add something new as draw out the implications of what the Shema means now that God's Empire has come.

Now that God's Empire has come in Jesus, Israel's love cannot be parochial but must be as wide as the world YHWH has created. Leviticus 19:18 occurs in that chapter of Leviticus containing the well-known divine call: "You shall be holy, for I the Lord your God am holy" (Leviticus 19:2). Thus in its context this call to love the neighbor is part and parcel of the holiness that characterizes and is required of us by YHWH himself! Thus YHWH-centeredness and love of neighbor are not in competition with each other but are two sides of the same coin. As YHWH's love is as wide as his creation, so too must our love embrace the totality of those around us. "Neighbor" cannot be limited or self-selected; a neighbor is anyone whose presence and need makes a claim on our time, attention, respect, resources, and care, in short, our love (see Luke 10:25-37!).[104]

Judaism at the time of Jesus was a people who, though living in their own land, were vassals of a far larger, far mightier power, the Roman Empire. They chafed under that overlordship and longed for the day when YHWH would intervene and return to Jerusalem, ending their exile[105] and restoring Jerusalem and the Jews to world prominence and leadership. As they endured Rome's continuing

---

104 Though we are dealing primarily with Jesus and the gospels, the following (lengthy) quote from Scot McKnight on Paul and his relation to the "Jesus Creed" is worth noting: "Paul argues that to love your neighbor as yourself, from Leviticus 19:18, is (1) our only debt to one another and (2) is the fulfillment of the law because it sums up the whole law.   It was this text in Romans 13 that convinced me that not only did Jesus teach the "Jesus Creed" as an adaptation of the *Shema* (Mark 12:28-32), amending it by adding Leviticus 19:18 to the standard *Shema*, but expected his followers to repeat it daily — as they had repeated *Shema* at least twice a day since the days of Deuteronomy 6:4-5.

The question that I asked was not just how often Leviticus 19:18 shows up in Judaism from the days it was given until Jesus (for which there is evidence that it played a significant role), but what role it played for Jesus and for the early Christians. That Paul repeats the Leviticus 19 part here, and then also at Galatians 5, and then that it shows up in James 2 — in a letter that shows tension with Paul, and then everywhere in 1 John convinced me that the followers of Jesus not only incorporated love of others as central but repeated this as a "creed"-like statement on a daily basis. That led to my own practice of saying in my prayers before the Lord's Prayer. (I have to insert the statement into the prayer book tradition.)

What amazes me every time I think about what Paul says here in Romans 13:8-10 is that he thinks — as does Jesus — that the whole Torah (seen as ethical demand) is summed up in this one commandment: if you love your neighbor, you do everything all those other commandments are getting at. That's how central love was to Paul." (www.jesuscreed.org/?-cat=9&paged=5)

105 This sense that the Jews still remained in exile even after the return from Babylon is a key theme that N. T. Wright has recovered in his study of Jesus. See *The Challenge of Jesus*, Chapter 2, esp. 39-43.

rule, the Jews did the best they could bear witness to their loyalty to YHWH by maintaining their distinctiveness as Jews from all other peoples and nations. That is why they were so insistent on observing the "boundary markers" that set them apart from others – circumcision, Sabbath, and food laws. They tried mightily to remember and testify to the truth that they were God's chosen people and that God had blessed them with gifts and promises that he had given to no other people. As we saw earlier, there is a third piece to their calling that tended to be neglected, forgotten, or ignored.

That piece was God's intention to use the Jews to bring divine blessings to everyone else. Without sufficient attention to this third piece, the other two parts of the promise tended to turn in an inward, exclusive direction. The "boundary markers" were practiced as hedges against contact with or inclusion of outsiders rather than as invitations for others to consider and embrace this way for themselves and their families. Israel clutched the precious promises of God to her breast and clung to them at all costs. These promises, partially appropriated, became occasions for Israel to look down on others and exalt themselves.[106] Openness to and contact with those others, the Gentiles, became a mark of deviance and a challenge to Israel's exclusive relationship to YHWH. A challenge they had to be beat back at every turn!

Thus the first circle of "neighbors" whom Jesus sought to reach was his Jewish "neighbors." Those who had forgotten or ignored the call to be open and welcoming to their neighbors on God's behalf needed to be called back to their roots in the Abrahamic call and covenant (Genesis 12:1-3). In other words, Israel itself needed to be reconstituted as God's people, those through whom God would spread his blessings everywhere and to everyone.

This reconstitution of God's people is the burden of Jesus' earthly ministry. That is why even though he is clearly interested in, occasionally reaches out to, and envisions the Gentiles as part

---

106 While this is certainly an understandable response on the part of a subjugated people desperately trying to sustain and nourish their cultural heritage, it remains a decisive deviation from who and what the Jews were called to be.

of his people and heirs to the Empire of God, Jesus himself, in a text rather embarrassing at first blush, tells his disciples whom he is sending out in mission, "Go nowhere among the Gentiles, and enter no town of the Samaritans, but go rather to the lost sheep of the house of Israel. As you go, proclaim the good news, 'The Empire of heaven has come near'" (Matthew 10:5-7). More on this in the next chapter.

The Jesus Creed, then, is central to reconstituting the followers of Jesus as the people of Abraham, the people whose commission is nothing less than to spread God's blessings to everyone! Jesus added Leviticus 19:18 to the *Shema* in order to remind a forgetful, neglectful people of who they actually are and what they are to be about in the world, that is, their true spirituality. A necessary clarification in the times in which Jesus lived and ministered – and today!

THE LORD'S PRAYER – JESUS' PRAYER

As with the *Shema*, so also with the *Kaddish* – Jesus modifies it too in light of the dawning presence of the Empire in his life and ministry. His version, what we call *The Lord's Prayer*[107] reads:

Pray then in this way:
Our Father in heaven,
hallowed be your name.
Your Empire come.
Your will be done,
on earth as it is in heaven.
Give us this day our daily bread.
And forgive us our debts,
as we also have forgiven our debtors.
And do not bring us to the time of trial,
but rescue us from the evil one.

---

107 There are two versions, the more familiar one in Matthew 6 and a shorter version in Luke 11. We will work with the more familiar Matthean version.

Jesus makes two changes to the *Kaddish*. He prefaces it with the address, "Our Father" and, like his changes to the *Shema*, adds three lines that change the focus from God to us (vv.11-13). We will look at each of these changes in turn.

Jesus' addition of "Our Father" places prayer for his disciples into a context of new intimacy. Not only does Jesus open up his own prayer life with the Father to us ("Our"), but lying behind the Greek *pater* ("father") is the Aramaic term *Abba*. This familiar, intimate form of address to God (something like our "Daddy" or "Papa") was rarely used by Jesus' contemporaries. It was, however, characteristic of him. And it is this characteristic intimacy with God that Jesus invites us to enter and experience.

This is in accord with the prophetic promises of God's action in restoring and renewing his people to covenant faithfulness which Jesus was bringing to reality. Particularly important here is Jeremiah 31:31-33:

> *"The days are surely coming," says the Lord, "when I will make a new covenant with the house of Israel and the house of Judah. It will not be like the covenant that I made with their ancestors when I took them by the hand to bring them out of the land of Egypt—a covenant that they broke, though I was their husband," says the Lord. "But this is the covenant that I will make with the house of Israel after those days," says the Lord. "I will put my law within them, and I will write it on their hearts; and I will be their God, and they shall be my people. No longer shall they teach one another, or say to each other, 'Know the Lord,' for they shall all know me, from the least of them to the greatest," says the Lord; "for I will forgive their iniquity, and remember their sin no more."*

The underlined portions highlight the transformation Jesus effected with his first change to the *Kaddish*. In Ezekiel 36:25-28 God makes similar promises to his people:

"I will sprinkle clean water upon you, and you shall be clean from all your uncleannesses, and from all your idols I will cleanse you. A new heart I will give you, and a <u>new spirit I will put within you</u>; and I will remove from your body the heart of stone and give you a heart of flesh. I will <u>put my spirit within you, and make you follow my statutes and be careful to observe my ordinances</u>. Then you shall live in the land that I gave to your ancestors; and you shall be my people, and I will be your God."

Again, the underlined portions reflect this revolutionary intimacy promised to Israel and realized through Jesus of Nazareth. Both promises also contain the characteristic covenant promise of fulfilled peoplehood under God in the bold print. Covenant intimacy with God will then mark this people; it will be their hallmark, their spirituality, the very well from which they draw nourishment and strength to be and live as God's people. All this is packed into Jesus' use of *Abba*.

The transition from focusing on God and God's Empire to the needs of disciples parallels the transition from loving God to loving others in his version of the *Shema*. Though these petitions are for disciples' needs, the pronouns used are all plural ("us"). All are implicated in these requests, we ask for these gifts on behalf of the community. The final line of a paraphrase of the Lord's Prayer from the Omaha Boys' Club newsletter makes this point well. After highlighting the communal nature of the petitions it notes that from beginning to end the Prayer "never once says 'me.'"

This prayer is situated within Jesus' Sermon on the Mount (Chapters 5-7) in Matthew. This, the first of five collections of Jesus' teaching on particular topics, focuses specifically on "Life in the Empire of God." Up to this point in the narrative, after the birth story, Matthew has shown Jesus being prepared for his Empire leadership (baptism and testing in the wilderness), announcing the onset of God's Empire, and calling his first disciples for Empire service. The Sermon on the Mount follows detailing what life in this Empire in discipleship to Jesus and service to Israel's God entails.

This sermon emphasizes living the life of the Empire of God amid the other various Empires of the world. With this, of course, comes inevitable tensions, difficulties, and conflict. Yet the urgency and necessity of such display of a "righteousness that exceeds that of the scribes and Pharisees"[108]remains. Within this setting the Lord's Prayer functions as a request for the necessary divine provision and protection against the disobedience and lack of faith that did in the Exodus generation in the wilderness.[109]

The provision and protection requested in Jesus' prayer lies very near the heart of the spirituality that catalyzes Empire living. Scot McKnight says it well:

> Hanging our prayers on the framework of the Lord's Prayer will lead us to yearn that all will have provision, be granted forgiveness, and be spared temptation. What do these mean? We need to think our way back into Jesus' world by recalling that we have just petitioned the Abba about his name, Empire, and will. Our concern is with God's breaking into our history to make this world right for all of us. And that means praying for others so that they will have adequate provisions, spiritual purity, and moral stability.[110]

The Jesus Creed (and Prayer) taps the deep sources of strength and enablement that lie in the new intimacy with and access to God. His Creed and Prayer lift up God's Empire with it consequent focus on loving and caring for others and allowing God to format our priorities, passions, and practices in their light. Thus Jesus' Creed becomes our own Creed and we enter more deeply and intimately into the experience of *Abba's* love for us and for the whole world.

---

108 Matthew 5:20.
109 Jeffrey B. Gibson, "Matthew 6:9-13//Luke 11:2-4: An Eschatological Prayer?" at www.findarticles.com/p/articles/mi_m0LAL/is_3_31/ai_94330381/print?tag=artBody,col1.
110 McKnight, *The Jesus Creed*, 21.

CHAPTER 7

THE JESUS NEED: THE CORPS
OF THE GOSPEL

And Jesus came and said to them, "All authority in heaven and on earth has been given to me. [19]Go therefore and make disciples of all nations, baptizing them in the name of the Father and of the Son and of the Holy Spirit, [20]and teaching them to obey everything that I have commanded you. And remember, I am with you always, to the end of the age."
(Matthew 28:18-20)

EVANGELISM'S GOAL

Evangelism is about reaching people, people who haven't yet heard or responded to the good news about what Jesus has done for us and our world. But when we share this gospel with others, what are we inviting them to do? Jesus gives us the answer in our theme text for this chapter printed above.

His answer, however, is not the answer we usually give about what it is we do when we share the gospel with others. We are drawing close to the very heart of our difficulties with evangelism at this point. Jesus approaches people not as potential converts to a new religion, nor as folk needing assurance of their place in the afterlife, not even fundamentally as people with ills, afflictions, and sins they need forgiveness for and deliverance from. Now, to be sure, Jesus does cure our ills, relieve our afflictions, forgive our sins, and assure us of our ultimate destiny with him - thanks be to God! Yet, surprisingly, this is never the end (both in the sense of termination point and goal) of the matter for him. He typically assumes that the person healed, exorcised, or forgiven is now restored to the community of God's people again and is to be assigned a role in the reconstitution of Israel he is working to bring about. In other words, Jesus is ultimately interested in new recruits for his Empire movement ("disciples" in the language of our text)! To put it differently, we become part of the corps of the Jesus' movement to fulfill his need[111] for "laborers:"[112] "The harvest is plentiful, but the laborers are few; therefore ask the Lord of the harvest to send out laborers into his harvest."

We are to be the living exemplars of God's Empire, the "disciples" of God's Empire who are called to make other such "disciples" of God's Empire throughout the world. The question begs to be answered: Just what is life in this Empire of God to which we are to model and announce? Glad you asked that! Jesus answers just this question for those he has recruited for the Empire in his famous teaching known as "The Sermon on the Mount" (hereafter SM) in Matthew 5-7.[113]

THE SERMON ON THE MOUNT[114]

The SM is carefully crafted to clarify the three primary drivers of discipleship, or life in the Empire: our passions, our priorities, and our practices. These three "P's" are shorthand for the aspects of our lives that need to be integrated and working in harmony for growth to occur.

Passions: the drives and energies that move us to act.

---

111 This does not of course mean that Jesus treats us merely as instruments toward another end. Rather, his end is our fulfillment, our joy, our living as God intends humans to live and he knows that the journey to that fulfillment begins and progresses as we take up his call to be and live as his people serving his purposes for the world. If the "medium is the message" (Marshall McLuhan), then what we are called to be and do must be the fulfillment for which God intended us (both now and in the new creation).

112 Matthew 9:37-38.

113 In terms of content, "Life in God's Empire" would be a better title.

114 I am heavily dependent on the work of Glenn Stassen, *Living the Sermon on the Mount* (San Fransisco: Jossey Bass, 2006) in this section though I have adapted it at points.

Priorities: our deep convictions about the truth of the world and our place in it.

Practices, the things we do in light of our priorities and passions.

Each of these should move in concert with the other. This, I think, is something of what the Bible means by a "pure heart."[115] As not-yet-fully-redeemed people, however, we only occasionally experience such unity and harmony among these three P's. Much of the time, one or two or all three of them are pushing and pulling us in such different directions that we are sometimes tempted to give up and cry with the Apostle Paul: "I do not understand my own actions. For I do not do what I want, but I do the very thing I hate."[116]

In the SM's description of the kind of people we will become in God's Empire, Jesus lays out precisely:

- ✓ the passions (The Beatitudes),
- ✓ the priorities (light and salt in the world), and
- ✓ the practices (righteousness greater than that of the scribes and Pharisees [5:21-48], righteousness practiced before God [6:1-18], and righteousness toward possessions and enemies [6:19-7:12]
- ✓ that will come to mark his people.

Jesus embodies YHWH's dream and his own life is a demonstration of the truth of his message. He is the best commentary on the SM. That truth was affirmed in splendor at his resurrection on the first Easter morning, YHWH's thunderous "YES" to the life and work of his son boomed out from the empty tomb. Jesus graciously invites others into this divine favor, which he calls God's

---

115 The 19th century Danish philosopher-theologian Soren Kierkegaard wrote a book whose title encapsulates this perspective, *Purity of Heart Is To Will One Thing.*

116 Romans 7:15; or as Clarence Jordan put it in his *Cotton Patch Version* of the Bible: "The desire to do right is there, yes, but the deed, no. I simply don't carry through on my good intentions; worse, I fall into the habit of doing the bad things I don't intend." See text at http://rockhay.tripod.com/cottonpatch/romans.htm#chapter07.

Empire. They will be the prototype of the world that should have been and will yet be when all is said and done. It is folk like this, then, who fulfill Jesus' need for disciples and laborers to carry on his mission in the power of the very same Spirit who's anointing empowered him for his earthly mission. And it is folk like these we can expect to become[117] if we too say "yes" to his summons and sign on to be one of 'laborers" Jesus needs.

Now the SM bursts into life for us! No longer are we able to consider (and usually dismiss) it as a set of impossible ideals designed to show us how short we fall and drive us to rely on grace. Nor is it directives for how we will live in God's Empire in some other time or some other place (either the so-called Millennium or in heaven). Rather we discover the SM is a profile of life lived now in and for the sake of YHWH and his Messiah and the world YHWH so dearly loves! Jesus' teaching here unveils the passions, priorities, and practices of just such a life.

The Beatitudes (5:1-11) reveal the passions that will energize and sustain YHWH's Empire people through the trials and struggles of their vocation. The first four are God-directed.[118] "Poor in spirit" means a humility before God. I call this "empty hearts and empty wallets." Jesus' blessing embraces both spiritual and material poverty. Often they are found together, aren't they? YHWH is our only resource and the only one worth having for Empire living.

The second blessing ("those who mourn") rests on those who are saddened by deep concern or those "who see this suffering aeon (age) as it is."[119] A clear-sighted realism about this world pierces the heart of one who lives out of God's Empire. In a culture obsessed

---

117 This is the ground for a genuine notion of "downward nobility." As we seek the place of God's blessing as we find it in the Beatitudes, we will inevitably find ourselves moving "downward" into a simpler, "nobler" way of living (at least those of us who are at present "affluent.").

118 David Garland, *Reading Matthew: A Literary and Theological Commentary on the First Gospel* (New York: Crossroad, 1995), notes: "The first four also begin with alliterative p-sounds in Greek that can be rendered: 'Blessed are the poor in spirit, the plaintive, the powerless, and those who pine for righteousness." (54)

119 Rudolf Bultmann, cited in Garland, *Reading Matthew*, 55.

with happiness this blessing is profoundly and often painfully counter-cultural. As William Willimon says:

> For instance, depression may be a therapeutic problem for us. We live in an affluent culture that places many unbearable and trivial demands upon us. Depression may be a positive sign of progress for the Bible. In many prophetic texts, grief is the beginning of the creation of space, a first act of resistance against the status quo. The Bible may have nothing against depression, may even want to provoke depression. The Bible doesn't just build on human experience. It rearranges our experience and gives us a way to name our pain rightly."[120]

Jesus' weeping lament over Jerusalem (Matthew 23:37-39) is paradigmatic of this Beatitude.

The third passion that fuels YHWH's Empire people is full surrender to will of God (traditionally meekness). Jesus in Gethsemane, agitated[121] and sweating blood[122] in anticipation of his ordeal to come, struggling to surrender fully to his Father's will, embodies this agonistic passion.

The fourth and final God-directed passion is a thirst for justice. YHWH's dream of a *shalom*-based creation drives us to embody and implement that *shalom* everywhere and with everyone we can. Its absence strikes us as a lack of basic nourishment and nutrition.[123] Again Jesus is our exemplar: "But strive first for the Empire of God and his righteousness (God's passion for his dream of *shalom*) and all these things (life's necessities) will be given to you as well."[124]

---

120 William H. Willimon, *Peculiar Speech: Preaching to the Baptized* (Grand Rapids: Wm. B. Eerdmans Publishing Co., 1992), 14. Also found at http://books.google.com/books?id=xV52QhgD6tcC&pg=PA14&lp-g=PA14&dq=willimon+depression&source=bl&ots=EB1b_QgK-du&sig=lo70O2UsLU4ccTr73XjC2-CEUZM&hl=en&ei=OSB-4S4OMHYGvtwfTgrHrCw&sa=X&oi=book_result&ct=result&res-num=1&ved=0CA4Q6AEwAA#v=onepage&q=&f=false.
121 Hebrews 5:7.
122 Luke 22:24.
123 See also John 4:31-33.
124 Matthew 6:33.

In relation to others, the blessed ones according to Jesus are those who practice compassion in action (the merciful), those whom like Jesus have learned that God desires mercy and not sacrifice.[125] Compassion (to suffer with) is the essence of mercy. Its incarnational thrust drives toward ever deeper relationships, especially with those who have fallen, are suffering, or in need of kindness.

Those who seek God's will "first" and only, those of pure and undivided heart, strive to bring ever area of life under God's direction. God's dream of *Shalom* is the dream that captivates them, the passion that moves them, and the vision that directs their day to day living.

Further, such blessed ones know the things that make for peace and work to implement them wherever they can. They are aware, too, that being a peacemaker can unsettle the "peace" of relationships and arrangements forged on the order of anything less than YHWH's *shalom*. "Do not think that I have come to bring peace to the earth; I have not come to bring peace, but a sword,"[126] is Jesus' way of putting it. It is no surprise then that, just like Jesus, practicing the things that make for peace will often rob one of the "peace" of contentedness, of social approbation, even of a good reputation.

Folk who live like this or are willing to be remade to live like this, such are "blessed" in God's Empire. It is they who form the corps of disciples Jesus needs to carry on with his mission.

And since the world we live in is a disordered parody of God's intention, to live so focused on God and God's way is to invite incredulity, ridicule, resistance, and even persecution. Though not seeking such responses, when they come we embrace them, yes, embrace them. "Rejoice and be glad," Jesus says. Why? Because by such response we are assured that we are on the right path, that of God's former messengers, the prophets, who suffered similar mistreatment for their faithfulness to God's call! These are the passions of the Empire that move Jesus' followers to live as they do.

---

125 Matthew 12:7.
126 Matthew 10:34

THE PRIORITIES OF THE EMPIRE

The remainder of the SM lays out its priorities and practices. Jesus' declaration that Empire people are to be "salt" and "light" in and for the world, a "city set on a hill," sets the direction of their lives.[127] This now is their vocation and their priority. Jesus frames this priority with three biblical images. First, salt was used to bind covenants to highlight their permanence.[128] Secondly, light, light to and for the world, was the people of God's ancient and enduring vocation[129] Jesus, himself the Light of the world,[130] wants to shine through his people such that their "good works" will bathe the world in God's light as from a city set on a hill. This third image, "a city set on hill," is a biblical symbol for Jerusalem,[131] the place of God's inhabitation to which the nations were to come to receive divine counsel and instruction.[132]

The corps of people Jesus needs, then, are to be a covenant people in the midst of a dark and dying world, the light of whose presence and activity gives both hope and direction to all who will see and take their witness to heart.

THE PRACTICES OF THE EMPIRE

The Antitheses

Lastly the SM lays out the practices by which his corps of followers will prosecute their vocation. Three sets of such practices are laid out.[133] The first, which are usually called the "antitheses" because Jesus contrasts his authoritative teaching with what was said of old in the Jewish Law. They are practical demonstrations of what Jesus called the righteousness greater than that of the scribes

---

127 5:13-16.
128 Leviticus 2:13; Numbers 18:19.
129 Isaiah 42:6,7; note the parallelism of "light" with "covenant" in v.6.
130 John 8:12.
131 Isaiah 2:2-3.
132 See Garland, *Reading Matthew*, 59-61 for more on these images.
133 See Stassen, *Living the Sermon on the Mount* (Kindle loc.784)

and Pharisees.[134] These six practices inscribe the parameters within which and form the bases on which the "city set on a hill" will live in light-giving ways. We might say that here we are given "the politics of Jesus."[135]

Look at how Jesus says we are to live and indeed by the power of his Spirit will live. Remember that God never commands us to do that which he will not give us the power to do. So every command can be "turned inside out" as it were into a promise. Thus, as the corps of his disciples, we will live in such a way that:

- ✓ reconciliation is a reality experienced and not simply a religious shibboleth mouthed in worship;[136]
- ✓ respect for others leads us to exercise the greatest of care in relating to them as God's beloved creatures;[137] our marriages receive utmost attention and care;[138]
- ✓ truth-telling funds our social intercourse;[139]
- ✓ creative thought will be given to fresh and arresting ways to make peace in new and changing circumstances;[140]
- ✓ enemies will find themselves loved and cared for into new relationships with those they oppose.[141]

Genuine Piety

Practices which under undergird this Empire "politics" come next. How do we relate to God in order to practice such a way of life? Jesus addresses four basic matters involved in genuine piety:

---

134 Matthew 5:20.
135 The title of John Howard Yoder's influential book of 1972.
136 5:21-26.
137 5:27-30.
138 5:31-32.
139 5:33-37.
140 5:38-42.
141 5:43-48.

almsgiving,[142] the function of prayer,[143] the content of prayer,[144] and fasting.[145]

These basic practices of Jewish spirituality are affirmed by Jesus as practices for his Empire people. The point at issue is signaled by v. 1: "Beware of practicing your piety before others in order to be seen by them." Our light is to shine but it is to shine out from us to the world illumining God's character, love, and purposes for it. Too often, however, we divert the light from shining through us to shining on us, illumining our practice of faith for the recognition and admiration of others. Self-aggrandizing piety dims the light, and we have our reward (such as it is) in the attention of others. But we have "no reward from (our) Father in heaven."

We have no reward because genuine piety grounds its practice in the presence of God alone. He is the audience for our practice of piety. For each of these practices Jesus concludes with the same phrase: "and your Father who sees in secret will reward you" so we will get the point! The only remedy for self-promoting piety, it seems, is to root it deep in the hidden soil of a living and growing relationship with God. In such a relationship, we grow more and more captivated by the holiness and beauty of God. Our desire for the applause and recognition of others atrophies. And we wait in quiet communion with the Father for those words that alone mean anything to us: "Well done, good and faithful servant!"

As you can tell by the space given to the three practices, Jesus' concern for prayer seems central. However, giving alms and fasting also deal with fundamental aspects of our life with God in the world among his people. Almsgiving is concern for restorative justice, a way of dealing with poverty through a redistribution of resources. Created in the image of a God who in creation practiced abundant giving in all his creatures, we as his image-bearers are also to practice abundant giving such that no lack plagues God's creatures. In

---

142 6:1-4.
143 6:5-6.
144 6:7-15.
145 6:16-18.

light of the recent sociological study Passing the Plate,[146] with its discouraging portrayal of giving to meet the needs of others among North American Christians, perhaps we ought linger a bit over this practice of almsgiving before we move on.

After his teaching on the practice of prayer Jesus enjoins fasting on his followers. This practice, though it seems an impossible or inconvenient burden to most North American Christians, reminds us (overly) well-fed and fully provisioned believers, that our abundance is a gift to be shared. Fasting creates moments where we can bodily identify with the plight of the poor and hungry in such a way that we "feel" (if only for a moment and only by our choice) the urgency of their need and open our hearts and wallets and pantries to them.

Fasting in a broader sense, can be a discipline to deal with other trouble spots in our relationship to God too. For example, fasting from consumption, or criticism, or sexual relations with a spouse for a season, or anything else that gets in the way of our practicing life as the SM displays it seem appropriate extensions of Jesus' teaching.

With regard to prayer, Jesus teaches his followers not only about its place, commending the private room over the street corner,[147] but (as per his disciples' request) its content as well. In distinction from pagan prayers which were long on addressing God with every title imaginable (the "heaping up of empty phrases" in v. 7), Jesus teaches us to start our prayer with profound simplicity, "Our Father in heaven." If God be our Father, our Abba (see Chapter 6), there is no need to "butter him up" with other titles and names in hopes of gaining a hearing. And if we are assured of God's "fatherly" care and attention, we can stay focused on God

---

146 Christian Smith, Michael O. Emerson and Patricia Snell, *Passing the Plate: Why American Christians Don't Give Away More Money* (New York: Oxford University Press, 2008).

147 Clearly Jesus is not ruling out prayer in worship or prayer with others. The prayer he will subsequently teach his disciples begins, "Our Father," after all. He is ruling out what I call "publicity prayer" – that prayer motivated by the desire to draw attention to oneself, one's church, one's cause, indeed anything other than the One to whom it is ostensibly addressed.

and God's agenda more than our own needs and wants in prayer. While our needs and concerns are pertinent and are represented in the prayer Jesus teaches (hope, bread, forgiveness, and rescue), they are placed within the larger context of a passionate cry for the full measure of God's Empire to come.[148] By praying "Our Father" we reaffirm God as the One who redeemed his people (his "son"[149]) from Egypt and will again lead them out to his Empire by an even greater Exodus[150] through Jesus.[151] We thus reaffirm our commitment to be his Empire people, those through whom he spreads the blessing of that Empire everywhere.

Prayers for justice, adequate food, forgiveness (about which we will have more to say in the next chapter), and rescue embrace the crying needs of a Empire people and a world not-yet-fully-redeemed. But perhaps the most important (in part because most neglected in western Christianity) petition is that God's will be done "on earth, as it is in heaven." "On earth" – on this earth, terra firma; this old, broken, battered globe that sustains our physical existence as well as the new creation which will be our habitation throughout eternity. This is the point of it all, in fact: to participate in God's salvation and demonstrate here and now in partial, though real and substantial, ways the life that awaits us in full then and there. We need "on earth" seared into our minds and hearts to combat the instinctive and problematic dualism we treated earlier in this study!

This ringing affirmation of the centrality of God's Empire in the heart of the SM reminds us that Jesus is indeed telling how it should and will be for those who sign on to be his followers, the corps of the Empire he announces and inaugurates.

---

148 At the heart of Jewish daily prayer was a petition that God's Empire might come during the petitioner's life time.
149 Exodus 4:22.
150 Luke 9:31.
151 See N. T. Wright's brief but insightful study, *The Lord & His Prayer* (Grand Rapids: Wm. B. Eerdmans Publishing Co., 1996).

Surrogate Deities

The final set of practices in the SM focuses on issues that perennially seek to seduce us from primary loyalty to God's Empire and distort our witness in the world. Singled out here for special emphasis are greed,[152] serving our "stuff (possessions),"[153] our self,[154] and our enemies.[155] Even before considering what Jesus says about these concerns, just the fact that he singles them out suggests their importance for his Empire people anywhere and anytime. Struggles with these matters, though taking different forms in different times and places, never go away nor do we ever finally move beyond them!

Greed, or the "having and hoarding" syndrome (or should that be "sindrome"?), remains a persistent, pervasive, and perplexing reality in most of our lives. We have too much, eat too much, buy too much, and want too much. Yet, at the same time, we know of the crushing need that destroys the vast majority of God's creatures around the globe, we feel oppressed by the burden of keeping up and insuring all our stuff, and acknowledge how wonderful and even just it would be to live a simpler life. Still, "having and hoarding" continues to be our *de facto* approach to living. Greed distorts our discernment, corrupts our will, and makes the light in us darkness! When those outside the church complain that there is no difference between the lifestyles of those in the church and everyone else, the power of greed is largely responsible. Only "treasures in heaven" (work for the Empire of God) have sufficient countervailing power to reorient us in faithful and fruitful ways.

Our "stuff"[156] (*mammon* in the Greek) seeks our allegiance and even our love in direct competition with God. "Worry" or lack of trust in God's fatherly care, is the enemy's strategic point of attack here. Apart from active participation in the community of

---

152 6:9-23
153 6:24-34.
154 7:1-5.
155 7:6-12.
156 6:24-34.

God's Empire people pursuing Empire interests we feel alone and vulnerable in the world. And, in large measure, we are! It's up to us to provide for and secure our own and our family's existence and well-being. And about that we worry. . . and worry. . . and worry. The need to secure our lives eventually overwhelms our commitment to God's Empire and its agenda, reducing both the time and energy we have or are willing to invest in it.

A decisive break with the "having and hoarding" mentality and recommitment to a God who both knows and is more than willing to provide what we truly need is the only antidote freeing us from the hold of our "stuff." That antidote Jesus stated memorably in 6:33: "But strive first for the Empire of God and his "justice" (traditionally "righteousness"), and all these things (life's necessities) will be given to you as well." And it will produce lives of full but simple and supple joy because our focus is not on "having and hoarding" but "sharing and serving"! Yet there is no denying the wrenching difficulty of such a call for us affluent folk! May God have mercy upon us!

7:1-5 has occasioned no small amount of confusion and misapplication. Are we to make no discernments and discriminations about the shape of our life together? Is there no accountability in discipleship? Is "live and let live" to be our modus operandi in the church? Many have thought Jesus taught such in this passage (and most of us have wanted him to!). However, if we consult Luke's parallel version of this teaching, we find that in place of "judge" (krino in Greek), Luke (6:37) uses "condemn" (katadikazo in Greek). The sense of both versions seems to be "do not condemn so that you may not be condemned (in the end by God).

Jesus warns here against our almost inevitable tendency to place ourselves in God's position and judge the attitudes, motives, and behaviors of others. When we so place ourselves, we stigmatize and often ostracize those we judge as reprobate, condemned, outcast, beyond redemption. By foreclosing on them in this way we are both unable and unwilling to offer them forgiveness. Rather than condemning, then, we ought to attend to ourselves and our faults and flaws, the "log" in our own eyes, and leave the "judging" to God.

Ironically, by this exercise of this seemingly Godlike judgment of others, we put ourselves, as well as others, in a position where the genuine Godlike judgment, that of his mercy and grace and unlimited forgiveness, cannot be offered and received.

In a world beset by class divisions, divorces, ethnic stresses, the inability to extend forgiveness and embrace those from whom we are estranged only exacerbates our difficulties rather than healing them. Jesus tells us here that we are to be healers of hearts and relationships. That, of course, does not preclude but rather assumes an openness and accountability to one another that enables us to deal with each other's sins and failures in reconciling ways. In this way we can overcome the frequent, and frequently correct, complaint that too often the church is more about divisive legalistic moralism and condemnation than edifying and healing mercy and forgiveness.

Finally, we meet the most obscure and perplexing passage in the SM. "Do not give what is holy to dogs, and do not throw your pearls before swine." What in the world is Jesus talking about here? Stassen produces convincing evidence that Jesus refers here to the Gentile Roman Empire that seeks to seduce, lure, or coerce its inhabitants' loyalty and allegiance. We are to withhold that loyalty and allegiance from the empire, though, and give it to God alone.

The Roman Empire was well-known for projecting the image of benefactor and father-figure for its people. The *Pax Romana*, the Peace of Rome, blanketed the empire and offered security and prosperity for all under its aegis. This was as much propaganda as truth, however, because, ironically, this "peace" was ruthlessly enforced by the Roman military ("or they will trample them under foot and maul you!). This imperial claim, though, was, is, and will always be the claim of empires in any time and place.

Jesus counsels his people not to buy into such propaganda. Rather, we are to "ask," "seek," and "knock" as children of a good and generous father, the world's true Emperor, who will indeed provide for us all good things.

Failure of discernment in this matter has bedeviled North American Christianity. We have regularly mistaken or baptized the ideology of the American Empire as constitutive of or at least consistent with the gospel of Christ. More than anything else, this failure of discernment has gutted the integrity of our discipleship. Hoping that we would become a nation with the soul of a church, the reality is that we been a church with the soul of a nation.[157] And the results have been dismal! Listening to Jesus on this matter is of urgent and prime importance for the church in our time!

Greed, "stuff," moralistic judgmentalism, and false allegiance to the nation-state rather than God's Empire are perennial surrogates for God. Worry unlimited, desire unsatisfied, a sense of moral superiority, and an uncritical patriotism drive our embrace of these surrogate deities and put a face on the church and its witness that fuel sentiments like those reflected in a recent book title, *They Like Jesus but Not the Church*.[158] The corps of the Empire cannot accept such a face. Their Lord certainly doesn't!

Jesus concludes the SM with a stark parable about the foundation on which one builds. The choice is either sand or rock. The former will not support structures built on it when the storms come; only the latter will. Jesus' hearers must choose! For he is indeed the rock, "the cornerstone chosen and precious . . . The stone the builders rejected" which has become "the very head of the corner."[159] Like "living stones,"[160] then, the corps of the Empire must build or better, allow themselves to be built, on the cornerstone who is Jesus Christ!

---

157 Gregory A. Boyd, *The Myth of a Christian Nation: How the Quest for Political Power is Destroying the Church* (Grand Rapids: Zondervan, 2006). The sermon series on which this book is based can be found at whchurch. org/content/page_721.htm.

158 Dan Kimball, T*hey Like Jesus but Not the Church: Insights from Emerging Generations (Grand Rapids:* Zondervan, 2007).

159 1 Peter 2:6-7.

160 1 Peter 2:5.

Only then, and only as such, can we fulfill the command/ promise Jesus give his corps: to go and make disciples and implement Jesus' victory throughout the world.

CHAPTER 8

THE JESUS BLEED:[161]
THE MORE OF THE GOSPEL

After this, when Jesus knew that all was now finished, he said (in order to fulfill the scripture), "I am thirsty." [29]A jar full of sour wine was standing there. So they put a sponge full of the wine on a branch of hyssop and held it to his mouth. [30]When Jesus had received the wine, he said, "It is finished." Then he bowed his head and gave up his spirit.
(John 19:28-30)

"IT IS FINISHED."

When Jesus cried "It is finished" from the cross, what did he mean? The tense of the Greek word translated "finished" bears the sense of completion or reaching the goal. Thus this cry of Jesus means not that his life has ended but that his life has reached its climax and goal. And because Jesus is the one true and faithful Israelite, Israel's story has reached its climax and goal. Since Abraham was called to set right what Adam had messed up, if Jesus is faithful as Abraham's "seed,"[162] he also takes care of the universal problem and crisis of Adam's race, sin and rebellion against God.

Even more than this, though, Jesus' cry "It is finished" ushers us to the threshold of the Holy of Holies of Christian faith. With it we enter the presence of the mystery of God and the mystery of God's presence with us and for us in the living and dying of this

---

161 I know the notion of "Blood" is as suspect in some circles, often rightly so, as it is revered in others. I ask that you read this chapter with an open mind before you pass judgment its content.
162 Galatians 3:15-18.

human being, Jesus of Nazareth. "Mystery" here means not a problem we haven't yet figured out, but rather a truth about God that we would never figure out unless God revealed it to us. When Jesus cries "It is finished" the climax and culmination of God's plans and purposes is reached, "once for all" as the writer of Hebrews likes to remind us.[163] Jesus' dying (and being raised and ascending)[164] comprises the decisive moment in all of human history – Jesus' own life history, Israel's history, and God's history with his creation. Yet this event (or better, complex of events) is not now simply a moment of our past but rather remains a potent reality that continues to shape and impact life in our time and, indeed, throughout all time.[165]

THE MORE OF THE GOSPEL

By the "more" in the chapter sub-title I mean the inexhaustible and unfathomable depth of what happened to us and for us and indeed to and for the whole cosmos when Jesus died and was raised from the dead.[166] In his cry, "it is finished," we catch a glimpse of light inaccessible, an ocean of love unending, and a horizon of meaning that finally transforms our best efforts at understanding into praise and our praise into inexpressible and wondrous awe. That we even glimpse this mystery of the person and work of our triune God, who not only acts lovingly but is, in truth, love itself (1 John 4:16), is a first effect of that very love laying hold of us (1 John 4:19). No matter how much we think we understand of what happened that first Easter weekend, there is always a "more"

---

163 Hebrews 7:27; 9:12,26; 10:10,12

164 References to Jesus' death should not be isolated from his life and ministry nor from his resurrection, ascension, and Pentecost. I will use Jesus' "death" as shorthand for the culmination, continuation, and efficacy of his redemptive work.

165 The tense of the Greek verb tetelestai suggests an event completed in the past but with continuing effect in the present.

166 Theologian Thomas F. Torrance speaks of the "boundless significance of what took place in Jesus Christ" and of the love and gifts of God which are "quite unlimited," indeed "inexhaustible." He notes that the church father Clement of Alexandria saw the atoning work of God in Christ as having "a value that outweighs the whole universe." *The Trinitarian Faith* (Edinburgh: T & T Clark, 1993), 181.

that dwarfs what we presently comprehend. While for Jesus "it is finished," for us the journey is always "further up and further in."[167]

Paul says it best at the end of his grappling with God's ultimate plan and purpose:

> *O the depth of the riches and wisdom and knowledge of God! How unsearchable are his judgments and inscrutable his ways! 'For who has known the mind of the Lord? Or who has been his counselor? Or who has given a gift to him to receive a gift in return?' For from him and through him and to him are all things. To him be the glory forever. Amen.*

(Romans 11:33-36)

THE DEATH OF JESUS

What happened at the cross, where Jesus poured his life blood out as a sacrifice of love to God the Father and of God's love for the world (i.e."The Jesus Bleed), is traditionally called "the atonement." Atonement is obviously central to good news of the gospel. In fact, atonement describes what God has done to reclaim his creation gone awry and restore it on its rightful path in the direction of its true destiny. God intends to create a situation of "at-one"-ment with his creatures. "Reclaiming" and "restoring" are the foci around which atonement orbits.

The Bible uses a wide range of images and settings to describe what we call "atonement." Rather than a neat, and logically tidy "doctrine" of the atonement, these images are more like the facets of diamond that come into view as we turn the gem in our hands. To focus on only one or two facets or images, or to proclaim one facet or image pre-eminent above the others is to do injustice to this great biblical reality. I will do my best to capture the truth of these varied images throughout this discussion.

The cultural emphases we noted in Chapters 1 and 2 that play a large role in generating the *Incredible Shrinking Gospel* also impact and "shrink" our understanding of atonement.

---

167 C. S. Lewis

Immersed in a culture which valorizes the individual above all else, the most important question we can ask of Jesus' death is, to put it crassly, "What's in it for me?" Such a "monochromatic" view of what Jesus did keeps us from seeing larger dimensions and deeper significances of his death on the cross.

Such a monochromatic view of the effects of Jesus' death creates difficulties when the culture we seek to reach no longer possesses awareness of or need for that particular effect. Up till recent times our culture typically defined its "problem" as sin, to which the gospel message of forgiveness was an appropriate response. Over time, however, our culture no longer seems to think of itself as "sinful" and tends to see its "problem" as that of shame or meaninglessness. The gospel message of forgiveness falls on deaf ears and closed hearts because it no longer genuinely brings the "good news" of the gospel to bear on the place where people today live.[168]

Another tendency in our culture is to isolate the events of what we call Maundy Thursday, Good Friday, Holy Saturday, and Resurrection Day as "the atonement." This creates difficulties we have noticed earlier in this study. Can we jump from Jesus' virginal conception straight to his death "under Pontius Pilate" as the Apostles' Creed seems to? Is his death organically connected to his life or is his life simply a prelude to the really important things that happened that first Easter weekend?

No More "God with a Scowl"

One final debilitating cultural factor needs to be addressed. It skews discussions of Jesus' death right from the start. That assumption is that God is mad at us sinners and required some kind of payment for it, the death of his Son, to appease his anger, become well-disposed to us, and offer us forgiveness and acceptance. In

---

168 I paint with very broad strokes here, of course. Some people in our culture still do view themselves as "sinners" and will resonate with the announcement of God's full and free forgiveness. As a rule, however, our culture has indeed shifted as I suggest above.

short, God needs an attitude adjustment toward us and Jesus gives that to him! Let's call this the "God with a Scowl" view.

I suspect we have all heard this version of what happened in Jesus' death at one time or another. But think about the implications of such a view! In the first place, it places God against the scriptures! The much-beloved John 3:16 makes this crystal clear: "For God so loved the world that he gave his only Son, so that everyone who believes in him may not perish but have eternal life." Here, God's motivation for sending Jesus is purely and simply love. God's disposition toward us is that he is already for us, working for our best end, seeking to save us. God cannot be divided against himself!

God does not need to have an attitude change toward us or some kind of action to appease his anger and desire for punishment or vengeance in order to forgive and accept us. Whatever else we make of scripture's assertions of God's anger and wrath against sin, and such assertions are there and they are important, divine wrath must be closely integrated with divine love,[169] subordinate to it, and serve love's ends and purposes.

Not only does this "God with a Scowl" view place God against himself as we saw above, it places God the Father against God the Son. This violates the ancient theological principle that the acts of the triune God are undivided and that each member of the trinity is involved in the acts of the others. What this means is we cannot have God the Father mad at humanity while God the Son loves humanity and sets himself to save them even if that means having to act to counteract the Father's anger.

Finally, this "God with a Scowl" view pits God against us. If we doubt God truly and fully loves and accepts us, honesty, openness, and intimacy with that God will prove difficult if not impossible. If we posit a God whose anger towards us needs to be appeased, we can never free ourselves of that niggling doubt that this anger toward us sinners really has been forever extinguished. Intimacy,

---

169 If there is no passion, jealousy, hurt at infidelity, and intensity in a relationship, can it really be called love?

and hence transformation, will be neigh to impossible in such a relationship.

In light of these considerations, let us take it as given that the scripture is right - "God is love" (1 John 4:16). It is we, then, not God, who need an attitude adjustment or, better, a change in relationship to God. And in love, God the Father sent God the Son in the power of the Holy Spirit to effect that change through the Son's earthly life, ministry, death, and resurrection.[170]

The Apostle Paul says it as clearly as possible in 2 Corinthians 5:18-21:

> *All this is from God, who reconciled us to himself through Christ . . . [19]that is, in Christ God was reconciling the world to himself,* not counting their trespasses against them . . . [21]For our sake he made him to be sin who knew no sin, so that in him we might become the righteousness of God.*

Did you hear that - "not counting their trespasses against them"? Do you know what that means? Our sins no longer stand between us and God! Through Jesus' death our sins have been completely removed from our relationship to God. The sole issue now between God and humanity is Jesus Christ! And the goal of Christ's work is "reconciliation," bringing God and humanity to "at-one-ment."

Yes, God is love. God the Father loves us, conceived of and shared fully in the sending and ministry of God the Son to live, suffer, and die for love of us, and through the Son sent God the

---

170 "If the Father were not mercifully inclined toward the human race all along, why would he have sent his only Son into this world in the first place? Surely, a determination to be merciful and forgiving must precede and ground the sending of the Son into the world to die in our place. Surely forgiveness is not *elicited* from the Father (grudgingly?) by what Christ did on our behalf; it is rather *effected* by the Father in and through Christ's passion and death. So the picture of an angry God the Father and a gentle and self-sacrificial Son who pays the ultimate price to effect an alteration in the Father's 'attitude' fails to hit the mark." Bruce L. Mc-Cormack, "The Ontological Presuppositions of Barth's Doctrine of the Atonement," in *The Glory of the Atonement*, ed. C.E. Hill and F.A. James (Downers Grove, IL: IVP, 2004) 366 (346-66).

Spirit that he might be present with us and intimate in us in on-going loving union and communion. This is the bottom line for Christian faith. This is the God, the only God, who has made himself known in Jesus Christ.[171] Any other God, especially "the God with a Scowl" so prevalent even in the church, is a false God we must reject.

THE COURSE OF ATONEMENT

"It is finished," Jesus cried from the cross. The decisive moment has been reached. A threshold has been crossed. The world will never be the same again. All Christians agree with this. What has proven more difficult for us is to keep our thinking about Christ's cross rooted in its biblical soil. When we take the story of the cross out of its native soil and replant it in the soil of other cultures' stories and images, distortions have arisen.

When we manage to keep to the biblical story line we learn to read the story of the cross in stereoscopic fashion. Out of one speaker comes the story of Israel and Jesus as the one true and faithful Israelite. Out of the other comes the story of the universal scope of Christ's death in the context of the church spreading into the wider Greek world. Each tells the same story even though each is modulated for a somewhat different audience. In one (roughly the Old Testament and the gospels) the focus is on Israel as the people chosen to bear God's blessings to everyone else. The universal note, the "everyone else" of Genesis 12:3, is often not explicitly present is implicit everywhere though its fulfillment clearly awaits some new movement of God. The story of Israel is present more implicitly in the second story. This does not mean it is not present there – far from it! The story of Israel continues to provide the grammar which keep this story and its meaning rooted in its native soil.

---

171 Philip Pullman beautifully narrates the death of the "God with a Scowl" in his *Dark Materials* trilogy.

```
┌──────────────────┐        ┌──────────────────┐        ┌──────────────┐
│ Speaker 1        │        │ Speaker 2        │        │ The Gospel   │
│ Story of Israel  │  ───▶  │ Story of Adam/   │  ───▶  └──────────────┘
│ Jesus as True and│        │ human race       │
│ Faithful Israelite│       │ Jesus as Second  │
└──────────────────┘        │ Adam             │
                            └──────────────────┘
```

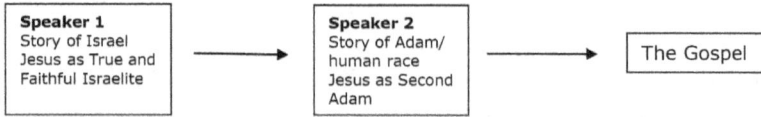

Thus though Jesus is clearly interested in Gentiles and envisions them as recipients of God's blessing,[172] in his earthly ministry he counsels his apostles to "Go nowhere among the Gentiles, and enter no town of the Samaritans, but go rather to the lose sheep of the house of Israel" (Matthew 10:5-6). His primary focus and mission was to reconstitute the people of God as a faithful vehicle of God's blessings. Jesus is the one to bring Abraham/ Israel's story to its climactic fulfillment!

Paul, on the other hand, is commissioned to take this Jewish story of God's plan and purpose for the cosmos to the wider Greek world. His focus is on the gospel's power to save "everyone who has faith, to the Jew first and also to the Gentile" (Romans 1:16). That he does just this is his genius! Paul looks to the wider aspects of the fulfillment of God's plans, even labeling the inclusion of the Gentiles among God's people as the "gospel" announced earlier to Abraham![173]

Another way to put it would be to say that the Gospels tell the story of Jesus as redemption achieved while Paul tells the Jesus' story as redemption applied. Paul's story, however, rests on the gospels' story of Jesus. Atonement occurred as the historical outworking of Jesus' life and ministry. He brings Israel's story to its climactic fulfillment. To understand atonement means to understand how Jesus' brought Israel's story to its conclusion. The plot line of Israel's story, you recall, is God's threefold promise to Abraham and Sarah:

- ✓ to get a get people through them
- ✓ to bless that people

---

172 See the so-called Great Commission in Matthew 28:18-20.
173 Galatians 3:8.

✓   to bless everyone else through that people

This is the story line atonement follows. It sketches a profile of what atonement means. It also counteracts the distorting cultural assumptions we noted above. Atonement is about far more than the individualistic concern, "what's in it for me?" It's about a people, Abraham's people. The effects of the atonement are multiple, able to address the variety of ways sin twists us. Atonement is the whole course of Jesus' life not simply the last three days or week of his life. This life in its totality, including the way it reaches back and embraces the lives of both Abraham and Adam, is the center and climax of all human history. Finally, the love of God is the motive and power of atonement. No "God with a Scowl" here!

THE COURSE OF ATONEMENT

Jesus' parable of the Mustard Seed in Matthew 13:31-32 is an apt metaphor for the course of atonement. The mustard seed, the "smallest of all the seeds" is planted in the ground and gradually grows into the "greatest of shrubs," indeed "a tree" in which all birds might come and nest. The farmer's preparation of the ground points to the Old Testament roots of atonement. This begins in Genesis 12 with the call of Abraham and Sarah and runs through the topsy-turvy story of Israel's history with God to the time of Jesus. As we have seen, this was a time of religious and political ferment born of the Jews' awareness that they were still in exile. Fired by the great covenant promises to Abraham, Moses, David, and Jeremiah's prophecy of the coming New Covenant, Israel was a tinderbox awaiting a divine spark to set it ablaze for revolution for the freedom and glory of its God and his people!

Jesus is of course the "seed." He is that "single grain" that "falls into the earth and dies" and thus "bears much fruit."[174] The first blooms of this planting signify the results of Jesus' ministry to Israel – to reclaim and renew God's people The branches that bear these first blooms stretch out to the skies with ever-increasing new

---

174 John 12:24.

foliage to provide a haven and a home for all the birds of the air. This pictures the effect of Jesus' atonement as his people fan out and set up outposts of his Empire throughout the world.

Narrating atonement as a story using the imagery of Jesus' parable is, I believe that most appropriate way to get a full picture of its scope and development. Atonement is a complex phenomenon with various layers and nuanced meanings. Jesus' death is the climax of his life, a life lived in full awareness of his heritage and vocation as Israel's Messiah.

Aware that he bore the mandate to live as an Israelite faithful to YHWH in every way, as Adam and Abraham/Israel had not, Jesus recapitulated Israel's (and Adam's) journey. He succeeded where they had failed. In short, Jesus gets it right! Jesus is both our representative and our substitute. He modeled what God called humanity to be. And in the course of living out that vocation he poured out his life in death out of love for his Father and the world that Father so dearly loves. Atonement thus entails Jesus' whole life as an individual and a representative/substitute[175] for all God's people. In love he bore the penalty of Israel's faithlessness - his murder on the cross by Jewish-Gentile humanity - so that God's love would reach out and reclaim them for him and for their divinely designed vocation. Yes, as he successfully recapitulates the failed effort of his forebears, Jesus gets it right! And that makes all the difference for us!

In the utter paradox of his unconventional performance as Messiah, his scandalous and repulsive death on a Roman cross and equally enigmatic and stupendous resurrection from the grave, Jesus brings to decisive climax and consummation God's purposes for his world through Israel. A first mark of this fulfillment was that those first Jews who followed this Jesus experienced what they could only call the true return from exile of God's people. Jesus had

---

175 Even some versions of penal substitution are valid here as long we don't envision an angry God ("the God with a Scowl") who seeks to punish Jesus because someone has to pay for our sins. Jesus bore the pain and suffering God's faithless people deserved by taking their place, a mission he undertook because he and the Father were united in heart and in love for the world.

defeated their true enemy (the devil), rebuilt a new temple (his own resurrected body), and reestablished Israel as pre-eminent among the world's peoples. This pre-eminence, however, was henceforth, characterized by suffering service to the last, the least, and the lost rather than privilege, power, and wealth!

Newly graced as God's new and true Israel, this community learned to identify itself as the people of Abraham, the people of promise, the promise of the world's redemption. As Abraham's children, they take this "gospel" of the world's coming restoration and of everyone's inclusion in it to the world. This is evangelism and, naturally, this became their reason for being. These new communities of Jesus' followers, those first blooms of his atoning life and death, spread out from Jerusalem and Judea to form the outer branches and foliage of the tree that will ultimately host the whole human family.

How can we account for the transformation of timid, uncomprehending, faithless deserters of Jesus into communities of disciples who were "turning the world upside down" (Acts 17:6)? To answer this question is to penetrate to the heart of what happened by virtue of Jesus' atonement.

Jesus' resurrection from the dead convinced his followers that all God's enemies have been put to rout. They were now sure that what they had witnessed throughout Jesus' ministry had indeed been God's powerful work to defeat all his foes and undo the consequences of their malignant Empire of terror. Jesus' mighty acts of healing, exorcism, forgiveness, his nature miracles, and his authoritative teaching all constitute assaults on this empire of evil. Moreover, God raised him from the dead, dethroning the greatest tyrant of all — the demon of death itself! Best of all, these followers had themselves been liberated from fear of both death and failure and found in the Risen One grace and power to live now in unprecedented and unimaginable ways. The power at work in Jesus and the Empire he inaugurated proved far more than a match for the pretenders and wannabes who imagined themselves at the head of their own Empires!

Yet we must remind ourselves that the power that routed and still routs the forces of evil subverts our very notions of power and victory themselves. Our strategy is to love the world into the arms of God. Both its victims and victimizers need liberating from themselves and the powers and forces of the devil. Our lives are our currency. We spend them in the service of others, even pouring ourselves out to death if need be. We carry no weapon save a message of good news. As the Apostle Paul put it:

> *The world doesn't fight fair. But we don't live or fight our battles that way—never have and never will. The tools of our trade aren't for marketing or manipulation, but they are for demolishing that entire massively corrupt culture. We use our powerful God-tools for smashing warped philosophies, tearing down barriers erected against the truth of God, fitting every loose thought and emotion and impulse into the structure of life shaped by Christ. Our tools are ready at hand for clearing the ground of every obstruction and building lives of obedience into maturity.*[176]

Key to the transformation of the disciple band into such a "fighting force"[177] is the certainty that their foes were already defeated. They were on the winning side. Mennonite theologian John Howard Yoder says it well:

> *The point that (the victory of Jesus) makes is not only that people who wear crowns and who claim to foster justice by the sword are not as strong as they think – true as that is . . . It is that people who bear crosses are working with the grain of the universe. One does not come to that belief by reducing social process to mechanical and statistical models, nor by winning some of one's battles for the control of of one's own corner of the*

---

176 2 Corinthians 10:3-6, *The Message.*
177 Remember the paradoxical, nonviolent manner of our conflict.

fallen world. One comes to it by sharing the life of those who sing about the Resurrection of the slain Lamb.[178]

Jesus gets it right! And in getting it right, his "might," as paradoxical, counter-intuitive, and impossible as it appears, makes right! He is Christus Victor, "Christ the Victor"! Confidence in him, and in him alone, created the vanguard of Jesus-followers who "turned the world upside down."

Finally, Jesus reconciles all things. This, as we have already seen, is the point of atonement, for humanity and, indeed, all creation to be "at-one" with the Creator and every other part of his creation. Through the atoning work of the birth, life, death, and resurrection of Jesus, he makes all things right!

On the largest horizon, Jesus' work culminating in his death and resurrection makes all things new — New Creation! Everything in God's first work of creation put out of joint, broken, or marred is put right again. As Paul puts it, "through him God was pleased to reconcile to himself all things, whether on earth, or in heaven, by making peace through the blood of his cross."[179]

This New Creation in Christ is now the reality out of which we live, even though it is not yet the full reality we experience in the world. Remember, we live in that "in between" time when the war has been won but the enemy continues to battle on, futile as that is in the end. The surety of final victory impels us to keep up with the struggle to spread that victory over more and more of the contested territory.

For us "in Christ" the territory we struggle for is the whole world.[180] Reconciliation is the form Jesus' victory takes in our struggle because the Reconciler himself is in our midst, in our

---

178 Quoted in Stanley Hauerwas, *With the Grain of the Universe: the Church's Witness and Natural Theology* (Grand Rapids, MI: Brazos Press, 2001), 17.
179 Colossians 1:20.
180 Romans 4:13.

community, indeed, in our hearts. He himself said "For where two or three are gathered in my name, I am there among you."[181] His triumphant presence in, with, and among us mandates and equips us to implement his reconciliation in the world in which we live. Indeed, Paul explicitly ties the two together in 2 Corinthians 5:

> *So if anyone is in Christ, there is a new creation: every-*
> *thing old has passed away; see, everything has become new!*
> *18All this is from God, who reconciled us to himself through*
> *Christ, and has given us the ministry of reconciliation; 19that*
> *is, in Christ God was reconciling the world to himself, not*
> *counting their trespasses against them, and entrusting the mes-*
> *sage of reconciliation to us. So we are ambassadors for Christ,*
> *since God is making his appeal through us; we entreat you on*
> *behalf of Christ, be reconciled to God.*

Jesus has restored the world, as we have just seen. Jesus has restored Israel to be the people of Abraham God intended them to be. Only now, this people includes believing Gentiles.[182] And this mixed body of Jew and Gentile, the "New Israel,"[183] reconciled to one another across the deepest and most primal divide imaginable, lives and shares the community for which God created us to ev-eryone they meet in the world.[184] Jesus has restored the personal wholeness we lost in the fall. We are now reconciled to ourselves. And Jesus has restored, or better, re-created, the cosmos we inhabit, fitting it out again to be our home for ever.

Jesus is, of course, at the center of all this. His cross and resur-rection won the victory as we have seen. His risen presence among us provides both the power and the model of reconciling living. This is the truth in the so-called "Moral Influence" theory of atone-ment. As his people, the church, we are called to live as he did, and does now through us, demonstrating the victory of his resurrection

---

181 Matthew 18:20.
182 "Everyone who does the will of God," as Jesus defined his "family" in
    Mark 3:31-35.
183 Galatians 6:16.
184 Ephesians 2:11-22.

over all the powers that seek to divide and destroy us; a "Community of Atonement" as Scot McKnight entitled his wonderful book on atonement.[185] Through him, we are made right!

Jesus gets it right. Jesus' "might" makes right. Jesus makes us right. That's the "Jesus Bleed." It's also the "more" of God's Empire, its never-ending display and provision of God's love for his creatures and his creation. It's also the tree of the mustard seed fully grown, hosting all the peoples of the world in its branches!

---

185 Scot McKnight, *A Community Called Atonement* (Nashville: Abingdon Press, 2007).

CHAPTER 9

THE JESUS SEED: THE SPORE OF THE GOSPEL

So when they had come together, they asked him, "Lord, is this the time when you will restore the Empire to Israel?" He replied, "It is not for you to know the times or periods that the Father has set by his own authority. But you will receive power when the Holy Spirit has come upon you; and you will be my witnesses in Jerusalem, in all Judea and Samaria, and to the ends of the earth." (Acts 1:6-8)

THE PROMISE FULFILLED

Jesus has died, been raised from the dead, appears to his disciples and, according to Luke, spends forty days doing additional discipleship training with them (Acts 1:3). During the course of this training the disciples ask Jesus a question that reveals we are still pursuing the agenda of the Empire of God. "Lord," they ask, "is this the time when you will restore the Empire to Israel?" (Acts 1:6). In other words, has the Empire of God now come and will we enjoy the benefits of living within that Empire?

It is crucial to read carefully here. Jesus does not tell the disciples they are on the wrong subject and refocus the discussion on the proper one. Rather he corrects their preoccupation with timing,[186] not with the Empire of God (v. 7). Jesus admonishes them to wait for the promised power of the Holy Spirit to come upon them and then to fan out through the world taking the good news of Jesus' victory to the ends of the earth.

---

186 Perhaps a word of warning for those disciples who today are similarly preoccupied!

That victory has indeed been won. Jesus' resurrection is God's imprimatur on him, God's approval and vindication of his obedience and way of life, of his announcement and implementation of God's Empire. With the gift of the Holy Spirit, Jesus mandates his followers to internalize and live out his victory and take that victory and implement it in all the world. In other words, they are to be about the work of God's Empire. Remember our earlier analogy from World War II: Jesus' decisive victory at the cross and resurrection is D-Day, yet his people keep on battling the enemy seeking to root out the remaining resistance until V-Day, Christ's return to fully and finally establish God's Empire (Chapter 3). The giving of the Spirit at Pentecost marks the onset of the period between D-Day and V-Day, the time of the church.

Jesus' victory, his resurrection from the dead, and the sure hope of his return, sets our agenda and provides us with the requisite resources to carry on the struggle. It is crucial here as well to maintain a "both-and" perspective - the "both-and" that holds together the personal and political dimensions of this world-shattering, world-shaping event. Marcus Borg and John Dominic Crossan, in their recent book, *The Last Week: What the Gospels Really Teach About Jesus' Final Days in Jerusalem*,[187] describe how claiming only the personal dimensions of Jesus' victory (personal transformation, the defeat of death, hope for the life to come) distorts "the good news of the gospel" (1:15).

✓   If the resurrection is not a victory over the powers (human and supra-human) that crucified Jesus and overturns their verdict that he is nothing but another "failed messianic pretender," then the cross remains an unmitigated and horrific terror. Death, or fear of death, stills rules and dominates the world. Our personal hope of surviving death does nothing to address its reign in an unjust and oppressive world.

---

187 Marcus Borg and John Dominic Crossan, *The Last Week: What the Gospels Really Teach About Jesus' Final Days in Jerusalem* (New York: HarperOne, 2006), 209-10.

✓ Without this victorious divine reversal of Jesus' judgment
and its proclamation of his defeat of the powers of evil,
destruction, and death, we remain trapped in a cynical
politics. The way it is in this world is the way it is, and
the way it will always be. In the next life things may be
different, but for this one the powers that be, the unholy
trinity of Mars, Mammon, and Me, call the shots.[188]

✓ Further, without the universal claims of God's victory
through Jesus' resurrection, we are prey to a sentimental
romanticism. Spring follows winter bearing new life,
chicks hatch out of eggs, new births succeeds deaths, and
the like, are among the familiar bromides we trot out at
Easter to try and explain Jesus' resurrection. Sentimental
romanticism, however, means we have given up on the
transformation of the world. These images suggest an
eternal back-and-forth between life and death, a tie, as it
were, between these two forces rather than the victory of
one over the other. Resurrection, however, means victory,
Jesus victory!

Finally, I would add, if the power and meaning of Jesus' resurrection are not decisive for all reality, personal and public, individual
and political, then it easily falls prey to our post-modern conceit
that "truth" only comes with a small "t." That is, truth is what I
believe, choose, or prefer it to be. The real mover in the world is
power. Whoever can enforce their view of things on others comes
out on top. Again we are left with a gospel that has no traction in
the larger world of economics, politics, and social issues.

Yet it is just to the larger world that Jesus sends his disciples in
the power of his Spirit bearing the good news of the God's Empire

---

188 Kathleen Norris, in *Acedia & Me A Marriage, Monks, and a Writer's Life*
(New York: Riverhead Books, 2008) cites Carmelite Constance Fitzgerald
on the consequences of the failure to acknowledge the new world opened
to us by Christ's victory: "Even worse, we come to assume that these
conditons – injustice, poverty, perpetual conflict – are inevitable, the only
possible reality, and lose our ability to imagine that there are other ways
of being, of other courses of action."

for the sake of the world. A benediction of Richard Halverson, former Chaplain of the U. S. Senate, catches this centrifugal dynamic at the heart of discipleship:

> "Wherever you go, God is sending you; wherever you are, God has put you there. He has a purpose in your being there. Christ who indwells you has something He wants to do through you where you are. Believe this and go in His grace and love and power."[189]

The giving of that same Spirit that makes us Jesus' seed, his people, his family, also makes us his "spore." A spore is a "walled, single- to many-celled, reproductive body, an organism capable of giving rise to a new individual either directly or indirectly."[190] The people God sends into the world to love and serve him is such a "many-celled, reproductive body" given to replicate the new life they have received in others and embody the kind of community God intends and desires for all his creatures.

God's sending of a "spore"-like people into the world takes the fulfillment of his Genesis 12 promise to Abraham and Sarah a step further. Recall that promise and its three provisions – that God would get a great people through them, bless that people with his presence and land, and through them bless everyone else? Have you ever noticed how each of the four gospels in their own way replicate and expand just this dynamic? Think about it. In each gospel Jesus gets a people for God through his obedience even to the cross and his being raised from the dead by his Father; in each gospel Jesus' presence with this people is the blessing at the center of their life (see Matthew's Jesus as "Immanuel – God with us" theme and John's vision of Jesus as the new presence of God's "glory" with his people (1:14-18); and each gospel ends with a "commission" sending them forth into the world to spread Jesus' Empire of God

---

189 Cited in *The Acts 16:5 Initiative*, vol.1 (Pittsburgh, PA: The Vital Churches Institute, 2005), 3-9.
190 Definition from www.dictionary.com.

movement (famously in the so-called "Great Commission" of Matthew 28:16-20).[191]

It's Luke's two-volume work, Luke-Acts, which reveals this dynamic most fully. He deliberately ties his two books together even though they were separated when the four gospels were grouped together in the New Testament. One way Luke indicates this continuity is by giving us two different accounts of Jesus' ascension, one at the end of the gospel (Luke 24:50-53) and the other at the beginning of Acts (1:6-11). The ascension adds a note of finality and completeness to Jesus' work as he returns to the Father in heaven to oversee the implementation of his finished work.

Secondly, in Acts 1:1 Luke writes: "In my former book, Theophilus, I wrote about all that Jesus began to do and to teach" (1:1).[192] His gospel story is only the beginning, then, of Luke's account of what Jesus has done, is doing, and will do in the world. The coming of the Spirit then, is the continuation of Jesus' presence with and power for his people.

We can trace the fulfillment and expansion/intensification of the three themes of the promise to Abraham and Sarah easily in Luke's work. He gives us an account of how through the birth, ministry, death and resurrection of Jesus God gets a new people, the first strand of God's promise to Abraham. The fulfillment, though, is also an expansion. Luke is the gospel writer who most stresses the inclusion of women, outsiders, outlaws, and Gentiles in God's new people. Here we see the fulfillment of God's very purpose in calling Israel – for the sake of the world. This one people, by God's unfathomable mercy made a prototype of what the world is to be, becomes God's vehicle, through the one faithful Israelite, Jesus, of many peoples becoming members of God's family.

The second strand of the promise is blessing, especially God's relationship with his people and land. Pentecost, the coming of the Holy Spirit in, among, and for God's people reflects fulfillment of

---

191 Though this passage has received some fresh readings in recent times that revision the thrust and character of this "sending."
192 New International Version.

the relationship part of this aspect of the Abrahamic promise. As with the first part of the promise, there is expansion and intensification in the fulfillment. Jeremiah 31 speaks of a New Covenant in which God will write his law on his people's hearts and each of them will know him personally. They will require no mediation in their relationship with God as in the Old Covenant. The gift of the Spirit is the realization of this part of the blessing.

Land too expands in the fulfillment of God's promise. God guaranteed Israel land, a place in which they could settle and order their lives according to his design. There they would reflect the light of God's intention for all humanity such that other peoples would notice and come to find out what was going on there (Exodus 19:5,6; Deuteronomy 4:5-8) - a kind of "Show-and-Tell," if you will. To be this kind of people at this point in the unfolding of God's plan required the chosen people to be a geo-political entity, a nation with boundaries to police, resources to gather, relations to other nations to attend to, and so on. God's people were localized in one place, identifiable on a map.

With the death and resurrection of Jesus Christ, and the coming of the Spirit at Pentecost, however, all that changed. The people of God are now no longer a national, geo-political entity. And that's not because it is some kind of "spiritual"[193] body that is invisible and undetectable in real life, but because it is a different kind of polis or city. Multiethnic, multi-voiced, mixing all classes of people, present in every corner of the globe, committed not to their own interests but to the good of others, owing allegiance to no earthly power but God alone, this new city, the "City of God" as St. Augustine called it, exists as an identifiable community within the larger communities of their locale and the public life of their area. This new community was to be:

✓   a community that lives by different standards,
✓   an alternative view of the world,
✓   unfamiliar values and visions for life together, and

---

193 Remember our earlier comments on dualism in chs.1 and 2.

    ✓   committed to other purposes than those of the city or nation-state.

These local expressions of the "City of God," are God's new "Show-and-Tell"! Now though, instead of one place on a map, this people can found in every place the map marks, each a beacon illuminating God's will and way for human life for all in their neighborhood and city to see.

The Apostle Paul in Romans 4:13 reveals that Abraham and his descendants would inherit "the world." That's right, "the world." The promised land of Canaan was a type of the greater promised land of the world that God's people would ultimately inherit.[194] Thus our being sent to "all nations" (Matthew 28:19) to "make disciples" is in effect a new and greater Conquest,[195] the entry into and settlement by God's people of their land!

We can summarize this biblical story line like this: Jesus, the new Moses (Matthew), effects a new Exodus (Luke 9:31) that creates a new People (1 Peter 2:9) whom the risen Jesus, the new Joshua (Hebrews 3:8f.), leads on a mission to "conquer" the world (Revelation 11:15). This is the story we are a part of by grace and the story that now defines us and forms the horizon of our hope.

As the spore of God's Empire we "conquer" by demonstrating human life as it was meant to be and inviting others to share the new relationship with God we have found and take up their roles in the story of spreading that "good news" to everyone else. This is the way we spread divine blessings to the rest of world – the third aspect of God's promise to Abraham and Sarah!

As the spore of God's Empire we are sent into a world governed by layers of a byzantine bureaucracy enshrined in endless institutions and regulations that flatten out our lives in diluted

---

194 Remember Jesus' promise that the "meek" will "inherit the earth" (Matthew 5:5).

195 Garrett Green's comment, "God is the *one who conquers not by force, but by capturing the imagination of his fallen creatures*" helpfully reminds us of the nature of this "Conquest." Cited in Michael Frost and Alan Hirsch, *ReJesus: A Wild Messiah for a Missional Church* (Peabody, MA: Hendrickson Publishers, 2009), 50.

and desultory ways. As spore of God's Empire we inject a new organic form of life, dynamic and reproductive, into this living death. Howard Thurman's wonderful poem "The Untried Melody" expresses this quality of spore-life beautifully:

> *I will sing a new song.*
> *I must learn the new song for the new needs*
> *I must fashion new words born of all the new growth in my life*
> *– of my mind – of my spirit.*
> *I must prepare for new melodies that have never been mine be-*
> *fore,*
> *that all that is within me may lift my voice unto God.*
>
> *I must prepare for new melodies that have never been mine be-*
> *fore,*
> *That all that is within me may lift my voice unto God.*
>
> *How I love the old familiarity of the wearied melody,*
> *How I shrink from the harsh discords of the new untried harmo-*
> *nies.*
>
> *Teach me, my Father, that I might learn with the abandonment*
> *and enthusiasm of Jesus,*
> *The fresh new accent, the untried melody,*
> *to meet the need of the untried morrow.*[196]

We embody this dynamic and reproductive life in three forms – sign, servant, sacrament.[197] As God's seed, spores of his Empire, our lives, in word and deed,

- ✓ point beyond themselves as signs to God as our source and goal,
- ✓ point through their self-giving servanthood to God's way of acting redemptively in the world,

---

196 This poem can be found at http://www.inwardoutward.org/author/howard-thurman.

197 I don't know the original source of this way of putting it. I heard it in a lecture given by Charles Ringsma of Regent College in Vancouver.

✓   and point to themselves and their life together as sacramental foretastes of God's Empire in the here and now.

Tony Campolo tells a story about a Bowery wino named Joe who was among the worst of his kind. Converted at a mission service one night, Joe's life changed immediately and dramatically for the better. He worked for the mission untiringly, caring for the least and the worst of the city. He cleaned up drunks, fed them, mopped up their vomit, swabbed the urinals in the bathroom, and cared for them in any way necessary.

At an evangelistic meeting in the mission some months later, another wino stumbled down the aisle, repenting, crying out "O God, make me like Joe!" After several of these pleas, the mission's chaplain leaned over and whispered to the man, "I think you mean to say, "make me like Jesus," don't you? "Jesus?" the man blinked uncomprehendingly. Looking back at the chaplain, he said, "Is he like Joe?"[198]

That says it all, doesn't it? As seed and spore of God's Empire, his grace enables us to reflect his character and transmit his life to others. Through us the world beholds the face of God present in his world, calling to those who have not yet responded to the good news of his Empire, caring for them in sacrificial, self-giving ways, and constituting for them an experience of the life itself, the salvation, to which God calls them.

"Is Jesus like us?" The world has the right to ask (John 17:20-23). We have the privilege by God's grace to be such. May it please God that this be true for all of us!

Face of God, Favor of God, Feet of God

Though the image of "spore" has its value and is organic, it is not personal. I want to close this chapter by suggesting the personal impact of being "spore" for God's Empire. I just described the role of the church in terms of being a sign, sacrament, and steward of God's Empire. Here I want to bring these descriptors home in a

---

198 I heard this story at a conference Campolo spoke at a number of years ago.

more concrete way. Thus, I want to say that we are "spore," the sign, sacrament, and steward of God's Empire in that:

- ✓ through us people can see the Face of God,
- ✓ feel the Favor of God, and
- ✓ benefit from the Feet of God present and active to guide and help.

Commitment and devotion to Jesus Christ slowly remakes us so that we increasingly come bear his image, to "look" like him. Others begin to see the family resemblance in us. The religious leaders in Jerusalem noted this resemblance, even though they were hostile to the church. "Now when they saw the boldness of Peter and John and realized that they were uneducated and ordinary men, they were amazed and recognized them as companions of Jesus" (Acts 4:13). Being with Jesus so marked this pair with a new vision and the courage to announce that vision to others, that they were recognizably like him! In them and through them others saw the Face of God.

St. Augustine taught that we become what we adore. Nathaniel Hawthorne gave memorable expression to this insight in his story *The Great Stone Face*. The hero, Ernest, heard the prophecy of the Great Stone Face from his mother as a child. The Great Stone Face was a striking human visage etched in the cliffs near Ernest's home. The prophecy predicted that at some point in the future a human being would arise who bore the exact image of the Stone Face and would be a person of uncommon wisdom, insight, compassion, and leadership. Ernest was captivated by the Great Stone Face, but even more so by the prophecy. He longs for the fulfillment of the prophecy in his lifetime. He assesses every great and acclaimed figure who comes through the area. However, each of them in the end falls far short of the image projected by the Great Stone Face. They were distinguished only by their extraordinary pursuit of very ordinary and base ambitions.

Undeterred, Ernest rejects the allure of these successful and powerful figures, keeping vigil with his contemplation and adoration of the face etched in the cliff. When he grew old, Ernest developed a reputation for solid common sense and an uncommon bit of wisdom. People sought his counsel on all sorts of matters. One day, the town gathered below the cliff to hear Ernest address them. One of them, standing to side, saw Ernest in profile against the backdrop of the Great Stone Face. He suddenly cries out, "Behold! Behold! Ernest himself is the likeness of the Great Stone Face."[199]

Ernest himself had become what he adored. Through his commitment and devotion to the Great Stone Face he was transformed into the likeness of the figure for whom he most longed. So too, for us. As Paul writes, "And all of us, with unveiled faces, seeing the glory of the Lord as though reflected in a mirror, are being transformed into the same image from one degree of glory to another; for this comes from the Lord, the Spirit" (2 Corinthians 3:18)!

Further, our lives as "spores" of God's Empire allow those around us to feel the Favor of God. We live in a "Kansas-like" world these days. Words alone no longer suffice.[200] The world cries "Show me!" God tells us "Show them!" The One who sends us and those to whom we are sent both require a flesh-and-blood demonstration of the good news of the gospel. That is the litmus test for credibility. If others do not experience the good news, few of them will believe the good news.

That's why Jesus came in the first place. As John tells us:

The Word became flesh and blood,
and moved into the neighborhood.
We saw the glory with our own eyes,
the one-of-a-kind glory,
like Father, like Son,
Generous inside and out,
true from start to finish. . .

---

199 http://www2.hn.psu.edu/faculty/jmanis/hawthorn/stone-face.pdf, 23.
200 My blog, entitled "When Words No Longer Signify" (www.leeawyatt. blogspot.com), deals with this crucial issue.

We all live off his generous bounty,
gift after gift after gift.
We got the basics from Moses,
and then this exuberant giving and receiving,
This endless knowing and understanding—
all this came through Jesus, the Messiah.
No one has ever seen God,
not so much as a glimpse.
This one-of-a-kind God-Expression,
who exists at the very heart of the Father,
has made him plain as day.

(John 1:14-18, *The Message*)

Note well: Jesus came to be one of us so we might feel the generous, truthful touch of the Father. This is how he makes the Father known – by grace-filled, truthful deeds. Can we do any less for our world?

Finally, others will not feel the grace-filled, loving touch of the Father if we do not go to them. As such, we are the Feet of God, extending the Father's healing and gracious presence and power as far as we are able. Solidarity with a suffering world is a crucial mark of love. Dietrich Bonhoeffer grasped thus truth in the midst of the hell that was Nazi Germany. He wrote in his *Letters and Papers from Prison*, "Only a suffering God can help."[201] And only a people who stand in solidarity with those who suffer and are oppressed, only a people, that is, who go to those in need to struggle and suffer with them, only these live as the very Feet of God. Only these can help to relieve suffering and distress; only these can be the signposts to God's Empire that will give the credibility to the gospel that is rightfully its own.

---

201 Bonhoeffer, *Letters and Papers*, 361.

CHAPTER 10

THE JESUS FEED:
THE STORE OF THE GOSPEL

While they were eating, Jesus took a loaf of bread, and after blessing it he broke it, gave it to the disciples, and said, 'Take, eat; this is my body.' Then he took a cup, and after giving thanks he gave it to them, saying, 'Drink from it, all of you; for this is my blood of the covenant, which is poured out for many for the forgiveness of sins. I tell you, I will never again drink of this fruit of the vine until that day when I drink it new with you in my Father's Empire.'
(Matthew 26:26-29)

THE SUPPER ACCORDING TO MATTHEW, MARK AND LUKE

The first three gospels recount Jesus' institution of the Lord's Supper (Matthew 26:26-29; Mark 14:22-25; Luke 22:14-23). In the highly-charged setting of messianic expectation in Jerusalem at Passover time, Jesus took his disciples aside to share the Passover meal with him. He knew this would his last meal with them. One can easily imagine the excited yet somber atmosphere. Everything was coming to a head. The disciples can feel it. But to what end, they knew not. This was not an occasion for light banter or frivolity. Indeed, the words spoken there by Jesus were those he judged the weightiest and most important he knew – his last will and testament as it were.

Jesus set the context for these his last and weightiest words by evoking the covenant setting of Exodus 24. There at Mt. Sinai

Moses solemnized the covenant God made with the people. This covenant built on the covenant God made with Abraham which we considered earlier. With that covenant God obligated himself unconditionally and unilaterally to this people and their prospects, well-being, and success (Genesis 15). As a result of this divine commitment Abraham and his people were now God's people, solely by his grace. This was now irrevocably their identity and destiny. On Mt. Sinai the focus is different. God prefaces this covenant with an updated expression of his gracious initiative and unconditional commitment to the people: "I am the Lord your God, who brought you out of the land of Egypt, out of the house of slavery" (Exodus 20:1). Then follows the "Ten Words" (literal translation of what we usually call the "Ten Commandments"). These "Words" detail appropriate expressions and practices of gratitude to God for his grace to the people. These practices are directed first and foremost to the proper worship of God and then to the nature and quality of the grateful and gracious community God desires.

What is crucial to note is that these "Words" or "Commandments" are given in the context of grace. That is, they are not about earning or gaining membership in God's people. They are directions for living for and demonstrating to the world the God who liberated them from slavery and the life of grateful freedom God offers the rest of humanity through them. In other words, keeping these directives is about living out the liberation God has graciously granted them. The people may or may not do a good job living these directives out, but this a matter that affects the quality of their witness not their standing as God's people.

The Sinai covenant, then, is a conditional covenant. There are things the people shall and shall not do on pain of discipline by God.[202] If you envision the covenant with Abraham as a large circle, then the Sinai Covenant would be a smaller circle within that larger one. Its focus is narrower than the covenant with Abraham, though no less important. Witness to God's love in daily life must be borne; his love must be expressed in the patterns and practices

---

202 Proverbs 3:11-12; Hebrews 12:3-11.

of the people. This is a matter of no small moment. Yet it is not a matter on which God's commitment to his people or to achieving his purposes through them ultimately depends. That rests, of course, solely on his gracious love and mercy.

This covenant at Mt. Sinai was highlighted by a meal with God. But before that meal, Moses dashes the sacrificial "blood of the covenant" (Exodus 24:8) over the people to seal God's covenant with them. When Jesus declares the wine of the Last Supper "my blood of the covenant" (Matthew 26:28), the associations of that event with the earlier covenant must have been thick in that Upper Room. This meal was indeed a covenant meal, in fact, a meal of covenant renewal.

Jesus here, in the setting of the Passover celebration of God's great deliverance of his people, enacts the renewal of the covenant with his disciples. In that there were "twelve" of them, they symbolize the new reconstituted people of God who are to spread the blessings of God everywhere and to everyone!

The early church continued Jesus' practice of table fellowship as the context for their ongoing celebration of this Last Supper meal. Paul's reflections on the Corinthian church's practice of the Supper (1 Corinthians 11) clearly reflects this ongoing celebration as part of a larger meal, the Agape feast.[203] Luke similarly describes a community "devoted" to "the breaking of the bread" in Acts 2. Christ's gift of this regular meal together for his sake forms one staple of the "store" of resources needed for the journey of sharing in his mission.

In particular, this Supper habituates us into the biblical view of time.[204] The biblical way of knowing follows this pattern: remember God's future in order to re-imagine the past and, thus, live faithfully in the present. Faith too conforms to this peculiar configuration of time: God's future (the Empire of God) breaks into the present thereby reframing the past (the Old Testament story) to highlight

203 http://en.wikipedia.org/wiki/Agape_feast
204 After writing this section I discovered a similar argument in Tom Wright, *The Meal Jesus Gave Us: Understanding Holy Communion* (Louisville: Westminster John Knox Press, 1999), Chapters 9-12.

its true contours and meaning. This transcendent future and trans-figured past collude to evoke transformed living in the present. Thus faith engages this future (God's Empire) which intrudes into the present with the coming of Jesus and draws from it images and visions of God's future to live by. In light of this future the past is transfigured to reflect its true reality and together this future and this past ignite faithfulness to Jesus in the present.

The past, then, is never just what has come and gone. That is, the past is never merely past. Nor is the future just what has not yet happened. That is, the future is never merely the future. We will see more of the significance of this later in this chapter.

This is how we celebrate the Lord's Supper. Paul's summa-ry sentence in 1 Corinthians 11:26 puts it all together: "For as often as you eat this bread and drink this cup, you proclaim (pres-ent faithfulness) the Lord's death (the past transfigured in light of the future)[205] till he comes (the future whose reality already determines our appropriation of the past and anticipation of the future.)" In this way the central dynamics of the Supper are un-veiled: the *realization* of God's past and the *anticipation* of God's already-present-yet-still-to-come-in-its-fullness future. They create the conditions for our participation[206] in God's story. And this shar-ing in the life God offers us, is indeed the life of the risen Christ himself. This is why we call this Supper "a means of grace." Such is the power of this feast![207]

---

205 This is why we can remember the Friday of Jesus' crucifixion as "Good" Friday or "Great" Friday as the Orthodox call it.

206 Brad Harper and Paul Louis Metzger, *Exploring Ecclesiology: An Evangel-ical and Ecumenical Introduction* (Grand Rapids: Brazos Press, 2009), use the triad "recollection, participation, anticipation" (137).

207 In response to some friends carrying on about the symbolic meaning of the Eucharist, Flannery O'Connor, when asked her opinion, said, "If it's only a symbol, then to hell with it!" Something happens to us in the celebration; God does something to us through our renewed relationship with him. If nothing really happens in the Supper's observance beyond the imparting of some symbolic meaning, then, I for one, agree with O'Connor, "to hell with it!" Fortunately, as we have seen, such is most assuredly not the case.

THE SUPPER ACCORDING TO JOHN

John tells his story of Jesus quite differently from Matthew, Mark, and Luke. In his Upper Room scene Jesus does not institute the Last Supper. His earlier claim to be the true bread of heaven, the bread of life (Chapter 6), whose body and blood must be eaten and drunk to share in eternal life, serves that function. John uses the story of the Upper Room to develop further insights.

I mentioned earlier that the Last Supper incorporated Jesus' characteristic practice of table fellowship. To invite others to one's table was in Jesus' society an offer of intimacy and solidarity tantamount to accepting them as members of the family! I suggest that John crafts this scene of Jesus' washing the feet of his disciples with Jesus' practice of radical welcome and hospitality in mind. And he makes such a practice incumbent on them too.

Jesus performs this radical act of foot-washing in the context of a meal. This is the tie-in with his practice of table fellowship. The parable of servanthood he enacts, washing the disciples' feet, serves as Jesus' interpretation of the Last Supper as we find it in the other gospels. Jesus shows us in an unmistakable way what that meal means. Radical servanthood, welcome, and hospitality to and for everyone is the "etiquette" (if I may use that word) Jesus establishes for his Table. This, he is saying, is what it means to eat and drink the body and blood of Jesus. It's the life of God's Empire acted out right before our eyes!

> *After he had washed their feet, had put on his robe, and had returned to the table, he said to them, 'Do you know what I have done to you? You call me Teacher and Lord – and you are right, for that is what I am. So if I, your Lord and Teacher, have washed your feet, you also ought to wash one another's feet. For I have set you an example, that you also should do as I have done to you. Very truly, I tell you, servants are not greater than their master, nor are messengers greater than the*

*one who sent them. If you know these things, you are blessed
if you do them.*[208]

From this view of the etiquette of the table as radical welcome,
acceptance, and hospitality flows other features of such etiquette
that concretely embody what Jesus calls "wash(ing) one another's
feet."[209] I mention just four here.

1. Equality in friendship: since we are all invited to this table by
    our gracious Host, unworthy though we are, we can welcome
    and accept others as equals, even as friends, sharing together
    the bounty of a wondrous Host. The differences between us
    can, at this table, become gifts we offer to Christ through
    serving each other rather than sources of fear and mistrust.
    Truly no one comes to this table by right, merit, or status;
    one only comes by unexpected and unmerited grace. Thus we
    can gratefully receive our neighbor as we ourselves have been
    received.
2. Peacemaking: at the table we learn both how to make peace
    with our enemies and who it is who alone can so empower us.
    We come to table as forgiven sinners, prodigals all. Without
    forgiveness we can only chew one another up[210] as we strive
    and fail to face or deal with our sin, division, and failure.
    However, by chewing the bread of Christ's body at the table
    instead we discover new resources for pardoning that sin,
    healing those divisions, and resolving our failures in restorative
    and reconciling ways. All manner of violence can then be
    confronted and dealt with, the subtle and small as well as the
    large and overt. The table will make peacemakers of us, if only
    we expose ourselves to its graces.
3. Hope: as God's people, adopted into God's family through
    Christ, we continue to bear the promise to Abraham that

208 John 13:12-17.
209 Here I am drawing on my as yet unpublished paper, "Between the Font
    and the Table: Why Only the Sacraments Can Save Us Now."
210 Galatians 5:15.

through his and Sarah's descendants "all the families of the earth shall be blessed" (Genesis 12:3). Our lives, then, are suffused with this hope. Not a selfish hope just for ourselves, but an expansive hope, wide enough to embrace all creation (Romans 8:18-25). At the table we are nourished by this hope, strengthened to live with courage and vision rather than small-mindedly and hatefully in a cynical and violent world.

4. Stewardship: Jesus' use of common elements of bread and wine in this holy feast remind us that God is the Creator of all things and uses all things to make himself known. All creation is thereby blessed and sanctified. Misuse or neglect of creation, then, is the height of ingratitude to a good and generous Creator. Stewards of creation we were created to be; stewards of creation we can become again at Jesus' table. The bread and wine of communion are also manufactured products, the works of human hands and technology. Thus human labor, technologies, and products fall within our purview as God's people to evaluate and employ with prudence and wisdom. Justice and freedom are to be the hallmarks of our wise, stewardly administration of these aspects of creation. Only at the table, where we receive "the body of Christ given for you" and are sent out "to be the body of Christ in the world" do we learn how to be broken and given for the sake of others as stewards of God's creation. At this table we encounter the passion to set all things right that animates true stewardship.

When Jesus tells us that we too ought wash one another's feet, at the least this entails the practices of friendship, peacemaking, hope, and stewardship. Much more could be added here and I encourage you to do so. In this way you will be thinking along with the gospel of him who gave his body and spilled his blood for us that we too might learn to give ourselves for others and the world. This is the covenant God made with Abraham and renewed through the sacrificial death of his Son Jesus Christ that we celebrate in this meal. This is the covenant that we enter upon baptism

and which defines whose we are, who we are, and what we are to
be about in the world.

BABETTE'S FEAST

Isak Dinesen's wonderful short story, Babette's Feast,[211] displays the power of the table at work. The story centers on a small,
devout community along the bleak coast of Jutland. Babette comes
there as a refugee from political turmoil in Paris. Two kindly poor
women take her in and Babette serves the community there for
years faithfully pouring herself out for them. The women's late
father founded the congregation in the village, and they struggle
to keep it alive, though pettiness, dissension, and age threaten it
with impending extinction.

Unexpectedly but joyfully, Babette discovers she holds a winning lottery ticket. The sisters assume Babette will return to France
and take up a life of comfort and leisure. To their surprise, however, Babette orders the finest foods, wines, china and crystal from
France. She plans and prepares a sumptuous feast for the little
congregation on the occasion of the hundredth anniversary of their
founder's birth.

The church, though, has grown so legalistic and puritanical
that though they feel obliged to accept Babette's hospitality, they
do not like it. Thus they gather, sour and dour, at the table she has
set with such love, grace, and skill.

As the meal progresses, however, pleasures these folk have never imagined begin to entice them in spite of their strict piety.

A visiting nephew of the most prosperous member of the
fellowship – a cosmopolitan and sophisticated military officer,
thoroughly appreciates the feast. He declares its magnificence and
announces that only once has he experienced its equal – in the most
prestigious restaurant of Paris.

Odd things begin to happen around this table. Old grudges
are forgiven, new pleasures experienced, and by meal's end those

---

211 Isak Dinesen, *Anecdotes of Destiny and Ehrengard* (New York: Vintage
Books, 1993), 19-59.

originally unwilling guests are dancing together in the village street, despite their age and the chill of the night air.

Only then does Babette reveal her identity. Before the upheaval that drove her from France, she was the chef of that preeminent Parisan restaurant. Moreover, Babette had used up her entire lottery winnings to give this obscure village a feast they did not want – and in the process to bring about a reconciliation and joy they could have experienced in no other way.

Yes, indeed, the Lord's Supper is surely a staple in the "store" of provisions the Lord has made for his people.

THE SACRAMENTS AS THE "STORE" OF GOD'S EMPIRE

I mentioned baptism above and it seems appropriate to bring it into the discussion at this point as the church has from the beginning regarded it too as a rite of similar importance and potency as the Lord's Supper. So also today, baptism and the Lord's Supper are acknowledged by most churches in some fashion as distinct and distinctly important rites for the church to observe.

Interestingly, according to the Bible, passage through water and a meal structure the whole of world history, Israel's story, Jesus' life, and the life of the church.

- ✓ World history emerges from the watery chaos (Genesis 1) and ends with the great banquet of the Empire of God (Revelation 22:17),
- ✓ Israel comes to life through the waters of the Reed Sea and orients her life around the celebration of the feast of Passover,
- ✓ Jesus' life is bracketed by his baptism in the Jordan and the Last Supper with his disciples in the Upper Room and, ultimately, the great banquet in the Empire of God, and

✓ Christian existence likewise begins in baptism, is sustained by the Lord's Supper and ends at that same great banquet of God's Empire.

I have suggested elsewhere[212] the image of living "between the Font and the Table" as a way of conceiving our life in Christ that reflects and honors the pervasiveness and power of these two sacraments in our lives. They both serve as staples, indeed, the primary staples, in the store of God's provision for us. We have already teased out some of the ways the Supper resources us for service and mission in God's world above and reinforced that with the story of *Babette's Feast*. Let's look at the role baptism plays in our lives.

In the New Testament we can discern at least seven gifts of grace we receive through baptism. Here they are listed in the following chart.

Gift	Function
A New Parent	God the Father both fathers and mothers his children
A New Freedom	The old life is left behind, buried in the baptismal waters; the Font is a tomb in this respect
New Siblings	The community of the baptized; "whoever does the will of God is my brother and sister and mother" (Mark 3:34)
A New Name	The early church often gave new names, "Christian" names, to those freshly baptized
A New Inheritance	A promise of new life on God's new creation
A New Culture	The resources and relationships of the church provide the gifts and nurture the habits of a growing faith and equip one for ministry

---

212 Wyatt, "Between Font and Table," (unpublished essay).

A New Vocation   As the New Israel of God (Galatians 6:16) the church takes up Israel's vocation to be "a light to the nations" via suffering serv-anthood

Baptism, the action that initiates one into the church, is the mark we bear forever. Baptism is, as I like to call it, the beginning that never ends. In fact, the Christian life is n/othing more or less than living out our baptisms. We never outgrow it; we never cease relying on it; we must always remind ourselves of our baptism. Martin Luther, when under spiritual attack from the enemy, would place his hand on his head and cry out, "Martin, you are baptized!" and he could withstand the onslaughts of the evil one.

The Lord's Supper, as we noted above, is an anticipation of the great banquet of all creation in God's Empire in the end. In this ritual we experience *the end that has already begun*.

Picture the relation between Baptism and the Lord's Supper this way:

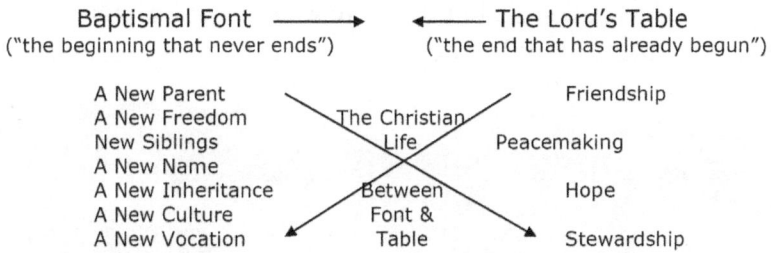

Baptismal Font ⟶   ⟵ The Lord's Table
("the beginning that never ends")   ("the end that has already begun")

A New Parent		Friendship
A New Freedom	The Christian	
New Siblings	Life	Peacemaking
A New Name		
A New Inheritance	Between	Hope
A New Culture	Font &	
A New Vocation	Table	Stewardship

Graces and gifts from both font and table follow their own dynamics. They intersect in the middle of the space between them, space I have designated as the sphere of Christian living. A sacramental life, nourished by regular reminders of baptism and celebration of the Lord's Supper orients us to live by their gifts and graces. This is the life:

✓ that as sign points to the Empire of God Jesus came to establish, and subverts the ethos and ethics of all other Empires and ways of life;

✓   that as a sacrament offers others a taste of the power and
    reality of that Empire; and
✓   that as a steward transforms us as we live it and enables
    us to erect signposts to God's Empire that offer a glimpse
    of the right ordering and the proper caring for others and
    the creation.

Baptism and Lord's Supper are means of grace, rituals through which we are incorporated into and sustained and nurtured by Jesus Christ himself through his Spirit. These sacraments create and grow relationships with both God and others. In baptism we are related to Jesus; in fact, *through baptism his life becomes ours!* With him we die, are buried, and raised to new life.[213] *Through the Supper* our relationship with Jesus is increasingly healed, deepened, and expanded such that *our lives, in effect, become his!* In the space between the Font and the Table, then, our lives are inextricably bound with his. We are, as the Apostle Paul liked to put it, "in Christ." And through us, the risen One is at work in our world implementing the victory he won at the cross over all the powers of the darkness, division, devastation and death! May we draw liberally from this generous divine "store" as we seek to live ever more deeply in the Empire of God.

---

213 Romans 6:1-4.

CHAPTER 11

THE JESUS DEED:
THE GOSPEL UNSHRUNK!

Now after John was arrested, Jesus came to Galilee, proclaiming the good news of God, [15] and saying, "The time is fulfilled, and the Empire of God has come near; repent, and believe in the good news."   (Mark 1:14-15)

A QUESTION

It's time now to sketch the big picture of all that Jesus said and did, which I call the "Jesus Deed." Let's begin with a question. What would you call a group that:

✓   lives by a vision and message of radical freedom and equality in a new society born out of the bondage, injustice, and oppression of "the way things are";

✓   looks forward to a coming age of peace, equality, and freedom;

✓   is especially concerned to do justice for the poor and oppressed;

✓   looks to a set of authoritative writings for guidance and insight;

✓   reads their history in a distinctive way;

✓   celebrates and remembers the lives of exemplary members of the group;

✓   lives in a way that distinguishes it from the larger community;

✓   meets in small groups to nurture their commitment to their vision and message, to one another and their way of

life, to plan future actions, and receive ongoing training
for their work;

✓ is single-minded and passionate about spreading their
   vision and message to everyone else; and

✓ recruits new members by befriending others, sharing life
   with them, inviting them to join in the work, explaining
   it to them, and, when appropriate, seek to help them
   become members?

What would you call such a group? During the Cold War era
we might have called them Marxists. In today's world we might
call them Al Qaida or some other revolutionary movement. At no
time any of us can remember, however, would we call such a group
"Church"!

JESUS – A COUNTER-REVOLUTIONARY?

Yet, if the reading of Jesus and his work I have proposed is
anywhere near the mark, "revolutionary" may just be the best word
to describe the movement he inaugurated. Indeed, my use of military imagery in earlier chapters hinted at this image. I suggest, in
short, that the "Jesus Deed" can best be imagined in our time and
place as a subversive counter-revolutionary insurrection against the
world's present but illegitimate rulers.[214]

Military imagery of some sort is necessitated by the big picture
of the biblical story from Genesis to Revelation.[215] Jesus comes into

---

214 This kind of imagery has been used before to describe Jesus but usually
   in an impressionistic fashion. I aim to use it as a substantive image that
   guides our understanding of who Jesus is and our life with him. In Latin
   American contexts and other oppressed situations Liberation Theologies
   have used similar imagery in recent times. However, our context in North
   America is of a different character and requires a fresh reading of the Jesus
   story for us. I would see my development of this imagery as a parallel effort to re-read the biblical story in light of the different forms of bondage
   and oppression that bind us. Such a reading is obviously related to and
   can draw from the various Liberation theologies but must address itself to
   the particularities of North American culture.

215 See Gregory A. Boyd, *God at War: The Bible and Spiritual Conflict*
   (Downers Grove: InterVarsity Press, 1997).

the world in order to win back the rule wrested from God by human and suprahuman rebellion and disobedience. This situation is not outside God's control, to be sure, but is a real situation to which God must respond. And he responds by sending Jesus as what I am calling a counter-revolutionary subversive to wage war against the usurpers. This is precisely what happened at Christmas according to C. S. Lewis. He writes, "Enemy-occupied territory – that is what the world is. Christianity is the story of how the rightful king has landed, you might say landed in disguise, and is calling us all to take part in a great campaign of sabotage."[216]

The very course of Jesus' ministry, in fact, suggests to no less a scholar than N. T. Wright a revolutionary movement. He writes about the Sermon on the Mount, "Remember who normally hid out in those hills. So when Jesus took his twelve disciples up there and gave them their marching orders, it would have looked a lot more like the founding of a revolutionary movement"[217] than any kind of religious meeting!

Further, Wright notes, when Jesus issued his famous "repent and believe" message, those words, in his time and place, meant not a religious revival service (as we in our time and place would likely hear them) but rather a call for all who heard him to let go of their violent revolutionary designs against Rome (repent) and follow him and his new, nonviolent way of defeating their pagan overlords (believe). Indeed, Josephus, a Jewish army commander, admonished various rebel groups in Galilee in 66 A.D. to "repent and believe in me" – the very same language Jesus used! He meant by this that these groups should relinquish their agendas for reckless violent revolution (repent) and instead, trust his, Josephus' way, of waging this fight.[218]

In another place Wright notes the character of Jesus' strategy in building his Empire movement.

---

216 *Mere Christianity.*

217 Tom Wright, *The Original Jesus: The Life and Vision of a Revolutionary* (Grand Rapids: Wm. B. Eerdmans Publishing Co., 1996), 53.

218 N. T. Wright, *The Challenge of Jesus: Rediscovering Who Jesus Was and Is* (Downers Grove: InterVarsity Press, 1999), 43-44.

We should not be surprised that Jesus in announcing (God's Empire) kept on the move, going from village to village and, so far as we can tell, staying away from Sepphoris and Tiberias, the two largest cities in Galilee. He was not so much like a wandering preacher preaching sermons, or a wandering philosopher offering maxims, as like a politician gathering support for a new and highly risky movement."[219]

These are among numerous indicators that when Jesus' story is read against its first-century Palestinian background,[220] Jesus' announcement of the Empire of God, his call for others to follow him, and his manner of leading and equipping his people strongly suggest that Jesus intended and those around him would have perceived his movement to be a radical religio-political-prophetic movement[221] forged in resistance to a corrupt Jewish leadership, their Roman imperial sponsors, and, ultimately, the dark lord himself!

This was not an unusual phenomenon in Israel in the period of 100 BC – 100 AD.[222] Jesus' movement as it turned out was more, much more, than these other revolutionary movements. But it was not less! Jesus intended at the very least a thorough-going liberation and reordering of the Jewish ethos and ethics under the rule of God with himself as God's sovereign messianic agent.[223] We misunderstand Jesus and Judaism in the first-century if we do not grasp this. And our gospel and our evangelism suffer mightily as well.

---

219 Wright, *The Challenge of Jesus*, 42.

220 For more of these indicators see chapter Two of Wright's *The Challenge of Jesus*.

221 Remember that there was no separation in Jesus' world between religion and politics.

222 See N. T. Wright, *The New Testament and the People of God* (Minneapolis: Fortress Press, 1992), 170-81 for details.

223 Two earlier classic works establish these points. André Trocmé, *Jesus and the Nonviolent Revolution* (Scottdale, PA: Herald Press, 1973) and John Howard Yoder, *The Politics of Jesus* (Grand Rapids: Wm. B. Eerdmans Publishing Co., 1972).

THE JESUS DEED

A brief review of earlier chapters shows how this image of Jesus and his followers grows out of those considerations.

Jesus' announcement and inauguration of God's "Empire" directly challenges the Jewish leadership, the Roman empire, and any other pretenders to sovereignty. This includes, preeminently, the dark and sinister power of Satan and his minions. This primal usurper animates the human pretenders and directly challenges Jesus for universal world power (cf. his temptations of Jesus, Matthew 4:1-13).

This latter challenge shows both the depth and power of the Empire Jesus brings:

✓ the satanic challenge he confronts is deeper and stronger than even the Roman empire;

✓ the remedy he brings cuts deeper and extends further than any human revolutionary agendas; and

✓ Jesus' revolutionary practice, though inscrutable and counter-intuitive to human revolutionaries, is more powerful and transformative than they could ever imagine.

The "gospels" of the various empires, Jewish, Roman, or satanic, promised only more of the "same old same old"; the "gospel" of God's Empire announces and produces something genuinely new, extravagantly transformative, and inexhaustibly hopeful!

Jesus as God's counter-revolutionary subversive takes his cues from God's agenda of dealing with human sin, individual and corporate. He envisions himself among that people who would bear God's blessings of shalom, utter well-being for both creature and creation, everywhere and to everyone. Jesus drinks deeply at the well of this "lore" of the gospel (Chapter 5). He takes on the mandate promised by God to Abraham and Sarah in Genesis 12:1-3. Through their "seed" God was to get a great people, bless that people, and bless everyone else through them. Jesus sees himself as that "seed,"[224] one faithful Israelite who will live out and fulfill this promise of world-blessing. Indeed, Jesus' life, ministry, death, and resurrection are "the" commentary on his fulfillment of this primary biblical promise.

The "core" of Jesus' gospel is a radical commitment to God's Empire. The famous twofold "Great Commandment" for Israel - to love God with all they have and are and their neighbor as themselves - and the prayer for God's Empire to come now and his will to be done on earth as it is in heaven are its chief expressions. God's Empire is all that matters; no divided loyalties here. Jesus' commitment to the sole priority of the Empire channels his passions and directs his practices to establishing that Empire among his people. This sole and single-minded commitment to one great end characterizes those we call revolutionaries. Such was and is Jesus, though far greater than any other revolutionary. So too shall be we who follow him.

As God's counter-revolutionary subversive Messiah, Jesus needs a "corps" of followers, fellow revolutionaries (Chapter 7). His first task after announcing God's Empire is to recruit disciples[225] (Matthew 4:18-22). After recruiting these followers, Jesus gives a classic exposition of what the subversive life in this Empire entails in the Sermon on the Mount (Matthew 5-7). It seems clear he intends this instruction (a New Torah) a practical guidance for revolutionary behavior, not some pie-in-the-sky platitudes, or a way of life only intended for the so-called Millennium, or a set of impossible ideals to drive us to a deeper awareness of our sin and need for forgiveness. This is what the revolution of the coming of God's Empire looks like on the ground in daily practice! Jesus is teaching his kingdom "corps" how to act and relate to others, themselves, and himself in this new age!

Jesus' death on the cross brings us to the "more" of the gospel.[226] Here perplexity, joy, wonder, and praise lend themselves to

---

224 Galatians 3:16.
225 Matthew 4:18-22.
226 Chapter 8.

adoration of the wondrous love of God for his children, wayward and ungrateful children, at that. Somehow, someway, from the depths of that special place in God's heart for us, flows an implausibly potent embrace of his creatures. Mercy came to us in the most unimaginable way – the birth of a Galilean peasant child, his improbable life, his death on a Roman cross at the hands of Jewish and Roman leaders, and indeed every other human being as well in our rebellion against God. There is more here, far more, than meets the eye, fills the heart, or can be captured by our minds. A verse from Charles Wesley's great hymn *And Can It Be* puts it well:

> *'Tis mystery all: th' Immortal dies:*
> *Who can explore His strange design?*
> *In vain the firstborn seraph tries*
> *To sound the depths of love divine.*
> *'Tis mercy all! Let earth adore,*
> *Let angel minds inquire no more.*
> *'Tis mercy all! Let earth adore;*
> *Let angel minds inquire no more.*[227]

This "strange design" played itself out in Jesus' counter-revolutionary subversion of the world's illegitimate rulers and their bastard rule. His radical prophetic effort to restore and reconstitute the Jews as God's counter-revolutionary corps (seemingly) ended at the cross. Jesus himself ended up hanging on a cross alone as the one true Israelite, faithfully following his vocation to the end, the bitter end.

The bitter end? Yes, the end of Israel, the final consequence of their unfaithfulness; the last, most horrific, unthinkably painful and humiliating exclamation point to God's failed counter-revolutionary movement! Yes, a very bitter end indeed.

- ✓ Death triumphed!
- ✓ The devil shouted with glee!

---

227 Words can be found at http://www.cyberhymnal.org/htm/a/c/acanitbe. htm

✓ And every other damned thing in the universe sneered in derisive delight.

Their demonic Empire continues on!

But they didn't grasp the "strange design" at work here (1 Corinthians 2:8). In the unfathomable alchemy of divine love, Jesus drank the cup of Israel's judgment to the very last drop. He bore the worst the powers that be could mete out to revolutionaries unwilling to submit and conform. Yet the Father's love forged a bond with the Son's faithfulness that vanquished them, even death itself. In the "mystery" of his Father's wisdom, Jesus lived the Father's love to the uttermost - "even death on a cross"[228] – and loved his children to life though they were dead in sin[229] and his creation mired in futility[230]

And

✓ Death dumbfounded died!
✓ The devil shrieked in horror!
✓ And every other damned thing in the universe slunk off into a hell prepared just for them.

New life transfigures all creation!

Jesus not only proved himself the Israel that Israel should have been and the Adam that Adam should have been. He did what he did for us, with us, and in our place. Jesus' death effected the full and final return from exile of his people, bestowing on all the great gift of forgiveness. Now they are free to live out their vocation as the people through whom God spreads his blessing. In his dying we are freed from ourselves for God, for each other, and for creation – reconciliation becomes the order of the day! His death turns every earthly power structure on its head. Death-dealing unjust and oppressive arrangements authored by rebellious powers and fallen humans are exorcised and that order is reversed into a new

---

228 Philippians 2:8.
229 Ephesians 2:1
230 Romans 8:18-25.

and life-giving–order. Finally, all things are and will be made new! New creation rules!

The "Jesus Bleed,"[231] his life poured out in service of the Father's love, is the revolutionary practice that accomplished his Father's counter-revolutionary plan. This same practice he passes on to his corps of followers by giving them his Spirit on Pentecost. The Spirit forms Jesus' counter-revolutionary corps into a movement of cruciform (cross-shaped) love that rules by serving the needy, loving enemies, and forgiving everyone.

All we can finally to say to such love, Charles Wesley said in the first stanza of his afore-mentioned hymn *And Can It Be*:

> *And can it be that I should gain*
> *An interest in the Savior's blood?*
> *Died He for me, who caused His pain—*
> *For me, who Him to death pursued?*
> *Amazing love! How can it be,*
> *That Thou, my God, shouldst die for me?*
> *Amazing love! How can it be,*
> *That Thou, my God, shouldst die for me*[232]

Cruciform love spawns a "spore"-like community capable of reproducing itself (Chapter 9). Jesus seeds the world by sending his people out to make disciples such as they themselves have become.[233] They reproduce by spreading the word of repentance and forgiveness (the commission to the disciples in Luke 24 and John 20) and serving others as Jesus had and does in Galilee (end of Mark). Word and deed! Proclamation and practice! This is how the counter-revolution continues.

Most human revolutionary movements are primarily concerned with doing, that is, changing the situation in which people live. Jesus' subversive counter-revolutionary movement of God's

---

231 Jesus' death always tacitly includes the resurrection, ascension, and Pentecost.

232 Words can be found at http://www.cyberhymnal.org/htm/a/c/acanitbe.htm

233 Matthew 28:18-20.

Empire, however, aims at a symbiosis of doing and being, that is, changing who we are, as well as what we do. In his "store" of resources for such comprehensive transformation are two very special gifts – the sacraments of baptism and the Lord's Supper. Both feed and nourish our critical needs of identity, intimacy, integrity, and identification.

- ✓ What we do (integrity) flows from who we are or believe ourselves to be (identity);
- ✓ who we are (identity) is rooted in the community we keep (intimacy); and
- ✓ those with whom we share intimacy largely determine those with whom we identify.

Jesus gives us a bath (baptism) that cleanses us. He also gives us new life, a new identity, and welcomes us into a new family. With them we share the intimacy of life together in and with this Jesus. He calls us to a new vocation or focus for our lives. We are to live now the life of the age to come, when God's Empire is established in its fullness. This means especially following Jesus in his characteristic activity of identifying with, welcoming, and offering hospitality to the least, the lowest, and the lost of our world.

Jesus also provides us with a meal for regular sustenance. Eating at this table sustains us with Jesus' own life. Gathering there often offers us a model of the kind of community God envisions for his world and provides opportunity for us to practice, as it were, the skills we need to live faithfully in the world: friendship, peacemaking, hope, and stewardship chief among them (Chapter 10).

AND YOUR CHURCH?

The "Jesus Deed," raises important and pressing if awkward questions as we seek to be faithful evangelists in our time and place. We must face them, however, if we hope to grow into that role and calling. These questions inevitably cluster around matters of the content, community, and commission of the biblical gospel.

Under both the "Incredible Shrinking Gospel" and the "Unshrunk" Gospel the community engendered and the commission under which the Christian operates are decidedly different. The former leads to what we earlier termed a "voluntary gathering of like-minded individuals" who see evangelism in terms of "saving individual souls" for eternal life with God in heaven. The latter entails a community chosen by God to replicate itself (make disciples) and bring divine blessings to the rest of creation.

So the question at this point is – can you envision a church, your church, any church, as a church living under the "Unshrunk" Gospel? Or as a counter-revolutionary force of King Jesus, as sketched in this book? I suggest this is the conceptual and pastoral rethinking and retooling that needs to take place if we allow ourselves to be conformed by the Spirit to the "Unshrunk" Gospel of Jesus Christ. Gerrit Scott Dawson envisions what might happen if we do:

> If the story and vision of the ever enfleshed Jesus can ever be recovered in the church, her people can be liberated from the shallow, enfeebling story of the currently entrenched consumerism. Then we can make our common way with others in this world, knowing that we are subversives. Christians are countercultural revolutionaries in the twenty-first-century west. We are spreading the customs of an alternative Empire. Neither withdrawing nor capitulating, and never imagining we can do it ourselves, the church engages the world with the gospel. It is a struggle to the death which leads to life, staged amidst ordinary lives as the citizens of heaven seek to turn the world's attention up toward a higher vision.[234]

What might all this mean for evangelism in the 21st century? I share my reflections in the last section of this book.

---

234 Gerrit Scott Dawson, *Jesus Ascended: The Meaning of Christ's Continuing Incarnation* (Phillipsburg, NJ: P&R Publishing, 2004), 161.

PART 3: REVISITING EVANGELISM

CHAPTER 12

WHITHER THE GOSPEL?: REFLECTIONS ON EVANGELISM IN THE 21ST CENTURY

OUR TRIANGLE RE-VISITED

Throughout this study we have been using this triangle to guide our reflections.

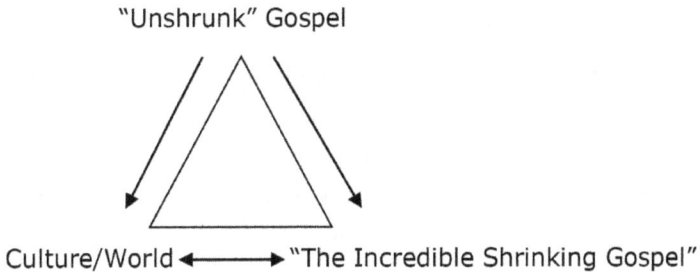

"Unshrunk" Gospel

Culture/World ←——→ "The Incredible Shrinking Gospel"

It reminds us that the gospel addresses and questions both the Church with its tendency toward an "Incredible Shrinking Gospel" and the Culture/World in its rebellion and unbelief. God calls the Culture/World to repentance and submission to him through the gospel. And God calls the Church to reflect on, critique, and reconfigure its "Incredible Shrinking Gospel" and learn to live in accord with an "Unshrunk" version of the gospel. This conversation with both the gospel and its culture is a continual ongoing process for the church.

At certain points, however, the corruption of the gospel in the church becomes so problematic that the process morphs from ongoing maintenance to full scale overhaul. I share the conviction of many others that we are presently in need of such an overhaul. My reflections here are intended as a part of such an overhaul of our understanding and practice of God's gospel.

"ORTHOPODEO"

There are several "ortho's" that have entered the Church's lexicon, like "orthodoxy" – right thinking or opinion or praise, or "orthopraxy"- right practice, or, more recently, "orthoparadoxy" – the truth of the gospel is paradoxical.[235] I prefer, however, the Bible's own "ortho" – "orthopodeo" which means "walking straight." It occurs only in Galatians 2:14 where, significantly, it is used in the context of walking in accord with "the truth of the gospel"! This connection with the "Gospel" makes "orthopodeo" especially appropriate for this study of evangelism. "Orthopodeo," then, suggests a double-sided process of reflection.

- ✓ Knowing how to "**walk** straight" requires active participation. We will only learn how to "walk straight" in the process of actually walking!
- ✓ Knowing how to "walk **straight**" requires thought and reflection to determine direction.

"Orthopodeo" is what I call the process of aligning ourselves with the gospel by the ongoing critique of our present understanding and practice so that we might better discern and set our feet in the direction of God's ongoing work in the world. This is the only context in which evangelism can be faithful to the Bible's God.

THE DOUBLE-FOCUS OF EVANGELISM

Evangelism, spreading the good news of God's Empire, is much more than memorizing a spiel outlining certain steps, Bible verses,[236] or prayers for others to listen to or share in. It is much more even than having a rich and profound theology of evangelism.

---

235 http://holinessreeducation.com/2007/10/05/orthodoxy-ortho-praxy-and-orthoparadoxy/
236 Things like "The Four Spiritual Laws" or "The Romans Road."

It is, rather, a way of life, a living demonstration of the gospel that can been seen, touched, tasted, felt, that is, experienced. Coherence between word and deed, theology and practice, faith and life, or "orthopdeo," is non-negotiable.

God's gospel pushes us in two directions at once to achieve critical relevance. One direction is the church's struggle to align itself with God's work in the world through continual reflection on and practice of what God's gospel is all about. In other words, we have to continually examine the shape of the church in light of the gospel.

God also pushes us to look at our culture to discern the issues, tension points, trends, and dynamics, which shape life for all who live within it. This dual-directional dynamic is analogous to the act of a child swinging. The child leans backward and at the same time kicks forward. Joy is born in this counter-intuitive action of going in opposite directions at the same time.[237] We must lean forward into the world at the same time as kick back into the gospel allowing God to reshape us into joy as we serve God and God's world in God's way.

Addressing these matters in light of the gospel allows us to discover the intrinsic and particular relevance of God's Word to life in our part of the world. It's a matter of learning to tell the same story as the rest of the church in the particular and distinctive way that allows the gospel to encounter our culture both in its strengths and its weaknesses. To be more specific, how does the gospel, God's counter-cultural subversive movement seeking to reclaim God's rightful rule over the world, view our North American culture? What would it focus on? Where is the heart, the nerve center, of this "Babylon"?[238] What are the dynamics that drive it? What is the place and profile of the church in our culture? If we do not attend to these questions, we make ourselves oblivious to the ways the ethos and ideas of our culture shape us. Then, instead of telling the same

---

237 Higher Ground Ezine at http://www.highergroundforlife.com/resources/ezine.pdf.

238 I've heard Tony Campolo say "America is the best 'Babylon' the world has ever seen. But it's still a 'Babylon.'" Just so!

gospel story, the "unshrunk" Gospel, differently, we end up telling a different story, "the Incredible Shrinking Gospel." And thus we betray the gospel!

Our New I.C.E. Age

In a warming physical climate, I believe, culturally, we are entering a new I.C.E. age. This is of course an acronym, which stands for three of the chief trends in our culture.[239] They are

1. Individualism
2. Consumerism
3. Experientialism

Notice first that each of these items ends in "-ism." They are legitimate and limited aspects of life that our culture has expanded into foundation stones, overarching principles, of life. Individuality, being a consumer of goods and services, and having experiences that touch and move us emotionally are good and necessary aspects of the creatures God made us. That we live by ourselves, for ourselves, and through our own power, billiard balls as we talked about in an earlier chapter, is another matter altogether. This applies to living to consume rather than consuming to live as well. The slogan "Whoever dies with the most toys wins!" has become emblematic of consumption distorted into a life principle. This is also the case with experiences when they too become a commodity to be pursued or purchased rather than a consequence of a life well lived.

---

239 Many call our North American culture of today "postmodern." However, "postmodern" means so many different things to different people and is itself a contested idea. I prefer to use my acronym, I.C.E., because it is different, refers to many of the same issues usually discussed as "postmodern" and doesn't bog us down in defining or defending "postmodern."

These "isms" have traditionally been called ideologies.[240] Recent analysts call them the "stories" by which we live.[241] This is helpful language. We live by the stories that have formed us more than the principles we derive from those stories.[242] We think of our lives as stories with turning points and changes like chapters. When asked who we are, we usually give some version, however condensed, of the story of our lives. We saw earlier how Jesus drew his sense of vocation and identity from the story of Israel as he had heard and learned it throughout his life. As for a story's power to shape us, just think of Jesus' embrace of the suffering and dying Messiah model for his mission. This story of how to be Messiah or a ruler was unknown in Israel, and unacceptable to them, or any other peoples. Yet, well, you know how it worked out – for Jesus, for Israel, and for all of us!

If we fail to heed the gospel's pressure on us to examine not only the culture we live in but the gospel we preach (the two downward arrows in our triangle) in and to that culture (the horizontal dual-directional arrow at the bottom of the triangle), we will end up with . . . pretty much what we have in North American Christianity today! The gospel we preach and live will reflect rather than challenge the I.C.E. Age culture we live in and keep what we call Christianity bottled up as simply a "religion," which as we saw

---

240 Ideologies are among the realities Paul calls "principalities and powers." Because I have focused on Jesus in this book I have not used this Pauline language. Jesus' confrontation with the powers of religion, revolution, and repression in his day are similar to what Paul means by "principalities and powers" in his day.

241 Two recent books reflect this way of analyzing cultural trends. James Bryan Smith, *The Good and Beautiful God: Falling in Love with the God Jesus Knows* (Downers Grove: InterVarsity Press, 2009) looks at the various stories about God in our culture that distorts the Bible's view of God and, thus, our experience of him. Steve Wilkens and Mark L. Sanford, *Hidden Worldviews: Eight Cultural Stories That Shape Our Lives* (Downers Grove: InterVarsityPress, 2009) reflect on larger cultural tendencies that impact us.

242 These stories obviously relate to and reinforce one another in a myriad of ways, though we haven't the space to discuss any of those interrelations here.

earlier (Chapter 2) means an activity that ultimately has no real impact on the world we live in.

What then might the gospel look like in our I.C.E. Age culture? Individualism reflects our desire to live independently, avoiding community, accountability, and liability for one another. We want to make our own way and life in this world unencumbered by the constraints of tradition, commitments, and relationships. As my three year-old grandson says: "I can do it by myself!" We hope to be self-made people. And self-made people always worship their makers!

The gospel grounded in life and conversation with our culture will of course critique this kind of individualism in a variety of ways.[243] But more important than the critique is the commitment of disciples to live together with one another in neighborhood and community, sticking with one another through thick and thin, supporting and caring for one another, being supported and cared for by each other, resources available for all from all, disagreeing and arguing yet not allowing such differences and arguments communi-ty-busters. In the creative tension of such community we discover who we really are, our genuine individuality, rather than the false self constructed in our autonomous search for self.

Such community is widely sought and longed for by many in our culture. They have discovered that the solitary search for self and meaning is futile.[244] They hanker for connection and belonging. Thus, the community of the people of God announced in the gospel (esp. chs.7,9) takes counter-revolutionary shape in our culture as itself a critique of the spurious "freedom" our autonomous individualism promotes and a living demonstration of the freedom and individuality for which God created us.

"Freedom" has become devalued in the West, diluted to mean only freedom "from" - freedom from any non-legal constraints on our desires and decisions. The gospel promotes a freedom "from,"

---

243 See Wilkens and Sanford, *Hidden Worldviews*, 27-43.
244 This is one of the reasons some thinkers believe we have passed or are passing from the modern era, which was built on confidence in such individualism, to the postmodern era which lacks just such confidence.

to be sure – freedom from sin, self, and devil, freedom from what hinders us in living the life for which we are created. Yet this life for which we are created is, at heart, a life lived "for," in commitment and submission to the will and way of God. This kind of freedom creates no inherent conflict with commitments, accountability, roots, traditions, or relationships. Ultimately, freedom is about the capacity to chose to "for" God and others. This is the freedom for which Christ set us free.[245] Such a full-bodied freedom-in-community will offer a winsome witness in our I.C.E. Age culture that, even though it longs for community, is so addicted to individualism that it cannot find on its own the reality only the gospel offers. Evangelism as the witness to the counter-revolutionary subversion and defeat of the world and its values by Jesus Christ embodied in genuine community bears profound witness to the One who is himself "the way, and the truth, and the life"![246]

Consumerism has so fully and successfully snagged most of us in this part of the world that it is, in effect, our default religion. This pseudo-gospel offers a creed ("I shop therefore I am"), a mission ("Whoever dies with the most toys wins!"), a set of "spiritual" practices (the actual processes of acquiring and consuming), a cathedral (the shopping mall), and a vision of the "end" (a life in which acquisition and consumption have filled all our needs and wants, erased worry from our minds, and set our lives in a land flowing with cash and comforts).

Our way of life starring ourselves as consumers is evident to all, easy to criticize, and seemingly impossible to escape. When those outside (or sometimes even inside!) the church claim that Christians do not live any differently than non-churched people do, I suspect it is our consumeristic ways of life they have in mind. Our priorities, patterns, and practices of consumption do not differ from theirs in any significant ways. A prerequisite to evangelism, then, is exchanging this way of life for one starring Jesus Christ as

---

245 Galatians 5:1.
246 John 14:6.

Lord and ourselves as servants to the world for his sake.[247] Easier said than done, I know!

That means conversion! Yes, conversion. A whole new way of life is necessary. In my pastoral and personal experience, people usually change for only three reasons (and simply knowing something is bad for us is not one of them): either we are coerced, hurt badly enough, or are captivated by an alternative vision. Well, our God does not coerce, so that leaves hurting badly enough and/or a captivating alternative vision. Both may be required for many of us to move toward sloughing off our consumeristic skins.

If we believe our basic posture toward life is that of a consumer, we lodge ourselves firmly in the center of our universe. Everything we encounter passes through the grid of "what's in it for me?" Have you ever walked out church and overheard someone say, "I didn't get anything out of that service"? That's religious consumerism. Or consider the oft-heard saying, "I'm spiritual but not religious." This too is version of religious or Christian consumerism. The "I" remains in the center and makes the decision as to the content and practice of their spirituality. This usually yields an eclectic type of faith picked "smorgasbord style" from established religions, philosophies, spiritual gurus, or our own intuitions or experiences. Such spirituality is usually tailored for the satisfaction of the believer's "felt needs."

Consumerism as a way of life operates on the principle that consuming constitutes our identity, our reality, and that our perceived "needs" take precedence over everything else. Thus, the slogan, "I shop therefore I am." Augustine, as we noted above, said that the human heart is restless till it finds its rest in God. For him, relationship to God constitutes our reality, our existence as human beings. We could alter the consumeristic slogan to read, "We worship therefore we are," to capture this point of view.

"I shop there I am." "We worship therefore we are." Two very different postures toward the world; two very different centers of

---

247 See Skye Jethani, *The Divine Commodity: Discovering a Faith Beyond Consumer Christianity* (Grand Rapids: Zondervan, 2009).

the world. The first has the individual "I" at the center. This "I" is active in establishing its own existence. And that activity is acquisition and consumption, a centripetal movement. The second has a corporate focus, "We." "We" are active too but in a very different way. This action is worship, a centrifugal activity that draws attention away from us and toward God. This effectively de-centers us and places God in the center of the world. It also makes clear the deepest issue consumerism raises – idolatry. Whoever or whatever sits at the center of our world, our "ultimate concern" as theologian Paul Tillich[248] famously put it, or that without which we cannot conceive of being truly happy, is an idol if it is not the true and living God.

Here's a key insight - evangelism is fundamentally about idolatry! The gospel is a challenge to our present loyalties and allegiances and a call to place our trust and loyalty in the true and living God.[249] Evangelism strikes at the very core of our lives, our fundamental bedrock commitments. Evangelism is not about morality, about how badly we live. Nor is it not about therapy, that is, how messed up our lives are, and that Jesus can make us better. That's true, thank God, but it's not the gospel! Evangelism, to say it again, is the announcement that the world's true and rightful Lord has won his counter-revolutionary struggle against all usurping powers. Liberation has come, now any and all can and should join this liberation movement to extend its boundaries "far as the curse is found, far as the curse is found."[250] Thus, evangelism is about who or what gets our adoration, loyalty, love, and commitment. It's fundamentally about idolatry, not morality, therapy, or any other benefits we receive from following Jesus.

Understanding evangelism as directed to our "ultimate concern" de-centers us. It pushes us to acknowledge who or what's at the center of our life. It challenges that center in the interest of faith in and following Jesus as one's true center of life. It invites us

---

248 Paul Tillich, *The Dynamics of Faith*, (HarperOne, 2001), 1-2.
249 1 Thessalonians 1:9.
250 http://www.hymnsandcarolsofchristmas.com/Hymns_and_Carols/joy_to_the_world-1.htm

to become the creatures we were created to be (i.e. "We worship therefore we are") and let God be God!

Experientialism is the last element of our new I.C.E. Age. We thirst for a never-ending series of experiences that shuffle and re-shuffle our emotions, sending them to their boundaries and beyond in search of a life well-lived. I call this the "Cat in Hat" syndrome. You remember Dr. Seuss' famous children's story, don't you? Two children sit at home on a wet rainy day with nothing to do while their parents are at work. Then the Cat in the Hat appears with all sorts of different and amazing spectacles that keep pushing the entertainment envelope and leave a swath of destruction in its wake. A cardinal sin in our I.C.E. Age is having nothing to do, which easily and quickly morphs into boredom. And boredom is never to be tolerated! The explosion of new media technologies beat back every threat of time with nothing to do. Affluence creates mobility which leaves fewer experiences or spectacles out of reach for many of us. Mobility decreases the importance and significance of locality, friendships, and commitment as we believe we can find satisfying experiences with interesting people wherever we want. Each of these experiences, however, raises our threshold of satisfaction, creating a need not only for another experience but a better, greater, more spectacular experience. And on it goes.

Such a way of living, centered upon our search for "life" by experiencing as wide an array of spectacles and wonders as possible, results in living "a mile wide and an inch deep."[251] This seems quickly to be coming the default mode of life in our time - breadth without depth, always deferring the question of meaning through an ironic[252] search for the next great entertainment. This restless and relentless quest for the next and the new fuels a situation in which, if we are not "amusing ourselves to death,"[253] we are condemning ourselves to life without depth, without roots which ground us in place and relationships.

---

251 The way one wit described the oratory of William Jennings Bryan.
252 Ironic because we suspect the search for meaning is finally futile.
253 Title of Neil Postman's wonderfully acute analysis of our culture.

Here too the gospel de-centers us and requires us to reconsider this way of life by experientialism/entertainment. The gospel calls and offers us a way of life, which though certainly vigorous, active, creative, and innovative, is grounded in "inner-tainment," a life of being rooted in the bottomless depths of God's love and mercy.

This "inner-tainment" is not our own achievement of course, it is by grace, as is everything in the Christian faith. And it requires us to allow ourselves to be de-centered, to submit to God in the service of his counter-revolutionary movement, to live and move, and even die, at his direction (John 21:18-19). It is a practical mysticism in which we learn together as a church to discern and follow the living Christ in the everyday ordinariness of life.[254]

This "inner-tainment" shapes the face of our interaction with the world. That is, "inner-tainment" is outer-focused. It is rooted in our affections rather than our emotions. The difference between the two is basically one of depth. The latter remain at the surface of our life and come and go with changing circumstance. The former are rooted at the core of our being. They are "the deep-seated dispositions, the settled and abiding postures of the heart, that qualify or color everything that we know or do."[255] They make us who we are.

Worship is a primary way our affections grow and are deepened. So also is the simple, daily practice of the faith.[256] No special spiritual heroics or regimen are required. No mountain-top experiences needed. If you have these kinds of experiences, that's great. But unless they root and deepen our affections they are of little lasting value.

What are these affections, particularly religious affections? Some of the primary ones are awe, humility, gratitude, a sense of direction, rightness, and well-being, contrition, mutuality and in-

---

254 Lee A. Wyatt, "Are We Having Fun Yet," *Journal for Preachers* (Advent 1994), 22.

255 Kendra G. Holtz and Matthew T. Matthews, *Shaping the Christian Life: Worship and Religious Affections*(Louisville: Westminster John Knox Press, 2006), 14.

256 2 Peter 1:3-9.

terdependence, obligation, delight, self-sacrificial love, and hope.[257] These form and set the direction of life that makes one a counter-revolutionary subversive in a still not-yet-fully-redeemed-world. Though by God's design and grace these affections do fulfill us and God's intention for the kind of creatures we ought to be, they also radically de-center us. We are freed from seeking self-fulfillment, self-actualization, or self-realization for ourselves in order to give ourselves to God and to others in sacrificial servanthood. Counterintuitive though it surely is, this is indeed the way to all these things. They are not achieved by striving for them, however, but by serving in the corps of Christ's counter-revolutionary liberation movement.

Each of these three I.C.E. Age features are centered on or have us at the center of life. That brings us back to the insight that evangelism is about idolatry and not morality, therapy, or anything else. Until we get the issue of who runs our lives sorted out, none of the rest of that matters anyway. The gospel is in effect a recruitment call – "the Lord Jesus wants you!" to serve in his counter-revolutionary liberation movement!

---

257 Holtz and Matthews, *Shaping the Christian Life*, 8.

CHAPTER 13

AND NOW ... HOW WE EVANGELIZE AND WHAT WE CALL PEOPLE TO (PART 1)

What is both Good and New about the Good News is the mad insistence that Jesus lives on among us not just as another haunting memory but as the outlandish, holy, and invisible power of God working not just through the sacraments but in countless hidden ways to make even slobs like us loving and whole beyond anything we could conceivably pull off by ourselves. — Frederick Buechner

THE CONSTRUCTIVE TASK

At every point when a culture changes, the church has at least three responsibilities regarding evangelism:

- ✓ to determine if there is a disconnect between the church and the culture it seeks to communicate the gospel to;
- ✓ to determine if that culture has distorted the church's message and ministry;
- ✓ and if so, to repent and ask for grace to generate a fresh expression of the gospel to share with our culture.

Actually, this should be an ongoing process, a continuous feedback loop in which the church is constantly scanning for possible distortions and fresh images and metaphors with which to address its culture. In truth, however, it is usually only when change forces itself on us that we go through this process in any thoroughgoing way. This is where we find ourselves today.

The previous chapters in this book represent my best effort to work through this process. Obviously, I find that there is a deep disconnect between church and culture in North America and see ways in which that culture has seriously distorted the church's message and ministry. I have also begun the work of repentance[258] and generation of fresh images and new forms of ministry. I want to draw that work into sharper focus in this chapter.

Our Focal Image and the I.C.E. Age

Church as the Counter-Revolutionary community of Jesus! That's my focal image for a fresh look at the message and ministry of the church. It arises out the biblical texts we have surveyed. This change in focal imagery then requires us to reassess our message and ministry in its light. So in this chapter we explore some implications of this new focal image for evangelism in the 21st century.

This image is not, of course, the only one the church might generate from this process. Nor should it be. God's people in different places in different cultures dealing with different dynamics and histories may generate different but equally valid focal images for their context. My claim is that this image of the church as God's Counter-Revolutionary movement captures the shape of the gospel in just the ways needed for the church in North America to reform and re-embody itself as the good news God always intended it to be.

Think again about the new I.C.E. Age we live in. Individualism, Consumerism, and Experientialism form the context for life in North America today. Theologian Christopher Morse accurately portrays the kind of life that characterizes our I.C.E. Age:[259]

- ✓ self-contained
- ✓ uninvolved
- ✓ dispassionate
- ✓ singular

---

258 In the literal sense of the Greek word *metanoia*, "to change one's mind."
259 Christopher Morse, *Not Every Spirit: A Dogmatics of Christian Disbelief* (Valley Forge, PA: Trinity Press International, 1994), 116.

✓ freedom as one long declaration of independence
✓ self-sufficient
✓ no need or willingness to admit need of others

In spite of growing awareness of the futility of such a life, and even some measure of cultural revolt against it, this way of living continues to fund our deepest aspirations and frustrate attempts to move in different directions. The figure below illustrates our dilemma.

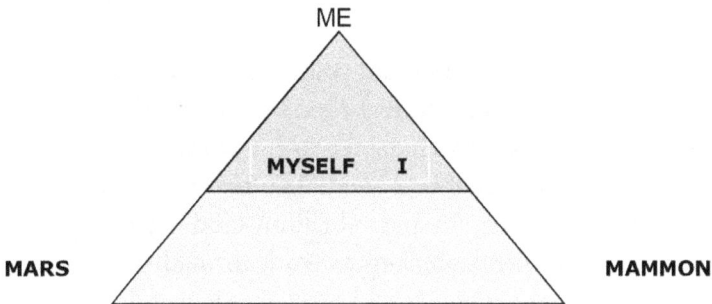

Individualism= Me
Consumerism – Mammon
Experientialism – Mars[260]

The "Me" serves as the shared point of contact between these inner and outer faces of the unholy trinity and anchors the inner face: "Me, Myself, and I." Following our first parents in the garden, we make ourselves the subject ("I"), the object ("Me"), and the agent of self-reflexive action ("Myself"). In other words, the cultural, outer face of the unholy trinity, our I.C.E. age, is generated by

---

260 "Mars" is the Roman god of war. War is one of the most profound of human experiences. No wonder we love spectacles, movies, games, and television shows that give us a vicarious sense of that experience. The recent hit movie Avatar is a case in point of how our moral imaginations gravitate to and cannot escape war-making as the experience that most deeply moves us.

our hearts which have been corrupted through sin to be "turned in on itself" (curvatus in se is the well-known Lutheran Latin phrase).

The Bible's God, the true and holy trinity, engages both faces of this unholy trinity, the inner and the outer, in his battle to reclaim, restore, and renew his creation and all its creatures. Evangelism is a chief weapon in this struggle.

God's Evangelical Counter-Revolutionary Movement

A community that is and does evangelism – that's perhaps the best way to reflect God's plan and insistence that in his people the medium and message should coinhere. It's been that way from creation onwards. Adam and Eve, God's representative image-bearers were to reflect God's character to his world by the way they cared for it and nurtured its potential and growth. After the great catastrophe of human sin and rebellion, God started again with Abraham and Sarah, promising to work through them and their progeny to bless the whole world. And that is the plan God is still working on through us. Jesus Christ has won the climactic and decisive battle of this struggle. We live on in the wake of his triumph, going forth as the "new" Israel[261] (Galatians 6:16) to implement Christ's victory in an ever-widening manner. God has equipped us and also expects from us the same coinherence of word and deed that he expected from Adam and Eve, Abraham and Sarah, Moses, and David.

Through the centuries this "evangelical" (gospel-centered) people has frequently been described by four "marks": one (unity), holy (purity), catholic (universality), and apostolic (rooted in the message of the apostles). I want to add a different set of marks here. Three of them come from the movie *Remember the Titans*.

Denzel Washington plays the new black head coach of a highly successful northern Virginia high school football team. These were the desegregation days of busing. The new coach faces many obstacles to get his black and white players ready to play together

261 Galatians 6:16.

for him. In one scene he is preparing them for their opening game. As the team run through drills he calls out "Who are we?" They respond, "The Titans!" "What are we?" the coach asks back. They answer, "Mobile, agile, hostile." Mo-bile, ag-ile, hos-tile – to that I would add frag-ile.

Mobile, agile, hostile, and fragile are, in my view, four essential marks of a community seeking to be and do evangelism in the 21st century. What do they mean? I suggest the following:

Mobile

We are a people:

- ✓ ready to move into a new future with the Lord;
- ✓ on the way, who do not ultimately draw our sense of identity or vocation from kith and kin but from the One into whose name we are baptized and the diverse community he calls to follow him;
- ✓ willing to forgo our own security for the sake of the Jesus we are following, the One who had no place to lay his head.

Agile

We are a people who:

- ✓ seek relationships, both within the community and with the world around us;
- ✓ accept and even embrace change and seek to ride the front edge of the wave;
- ✓ resist the lure of the spectacle which often renders us unable to act in meaningful ways as well as the token, often media-driven "actions" that yield little effect;[262]

---

262 Against the growing phenomena of "slacktivism" – "a portmanteau formed out of the words *slacker* and *activism*. The word is considered a pejorative term that describes "feel-good" measures, in support of an issue or social cause, that have little or no practical effect other than to make the person doing it feel satisfaction. The acts also tend to require little personal effort from the slacktivist" (see "slacktivism in Wikipedia, http://en.wikipedia.org/wiki/Slacktivism.

✓ like our Lord, are willing and able to bend the knee, take up the basin and serve one another by washing each others' feet.[263]

Hostile

We are a people who:

✓ serve a Empire that "comes violently";[264] and a Lord who came "not to bring peace, but a sword";[265]

✓ live and tell the truth, which, in a world built on lies and illusions cannot help but disturb the peace (we tell the truth especially about ourselves, thus we are a humble people);

✓ practice the "violence of love"[266] and are equipped by God with his own "armor"[267] and overcome the enemy by Jesus' victory at the cross, our own faithful testimony to him, and our willingness to even give up our lives serving him,[268]

✓ are called to be part of Jesus' Counter-Revolutionary movement, to live out a different life as we play our roles in God's Empire struggle.

Fragile

We are a broken people who:

✓ have found healing in Jesus Christ;

✓ continue to be a broken people who keep on finding healing in Jesus Christ (this vulnerability to owning our brokenness and receiving Jesus' healing touch enables us to offer others that very same comfort and healing as they face their own brokenness);[269]

---

263 John 13:1-17.
264 Matthew 11:12 (NRSV, footnote).
265 Matthew 10:34.
266 Title of a book by Archbishop Oscar Romero of El Salvador.
267 Ephesians 6:10-20.
268 Revelation 12:10-12.
269 2 Corinthians 1:3-7.

✓ are called to "bear our cross,"[270] to live as suffering servants, indeed even "Silent Servants of the Used, Abused, and Utterly Screwed Up"[271]

Such an evangelical community - mobile, agile, hostile, and fragile - is the community that actively engages both the inner face of the unholy trinity – Me, Myself, and I – and its outer, cultural face – Mars, Mammon, and Me. Both are key components of evangelism – remember the Newbigin Triangle![272] The church is always being reformed by the Word of the Gospel (the inner face of the unholy trinity) and challenged, critiqued, and called to wrestle with the demonic triad's outer, cultural face. What then do we do? What might evangelism look like in our I.C.E. Age?

Evangelism: Dialogue, Dignity, and Discernment

Dialogue

I think sharing the gospel in our time and place probably ought to begin with a confession. The profile of the church in North America is not very good. Sexual and financial scandals, cultural arrogance and spiritual impotence[273] (the two usually go together), authoritarianism, lack of genuine discernment, clownishness, the history of the church's bad behavior through the centuries – these kinds of things make some sort of acknowledgment and confession necessary. Shane Claiborne, in a recent article,[274] begins with just such an acknowledgment.

> To all my nonbelieving, sort-of-believing, and used-to-be-believing friends: I feel like I should begin with a confession.

---

270 Mark 8:34-38.

271 Thomas Klise, *The Last Western* (Argus Communications, 1974).

272 Chapter 1.

273 Lesslie Newbigin, *The Other Side of 1984* (Geneva: World Council of Churches, 1983), 23, notes that such impotence in the West springs from the churches' acquiescence in being relegated to the private sphere of life with no input to or impact on public life as the price of acceptance.

274 Shane Claiborne, "What If Jesus Meant All That Stuff?" *Esquire*, online at www.esquire.com/print-this/shane-claiborne-1209

I am sorry that so often the biggest obstacle to God has been Christians. Christians who have had so much to say with our mouths and so little to show with our lives. I am sorry that so often we have forgotten the Christ of our Christianity. Forgive us. Forgive us for the embarrassing things we have done in the name of God.

In more formal theological language, German theologian and martyr, Dietrich Bonhoeffer does the same thing:

> The Church today is that community of people who, grasped by the power of Christ's grace, acknowledge, confess, and take upon themselves not only their personal sins, but also the Western world's falling away from Jesus Christ as guilt towards Jesus Christ. The church is where Jesus makes his form real in the midst of the world. Therefore, only the church can be the place of personal and corporate rebirth and renewal ... The Church confesses that it has not professed openly and clearly enough its message of the one God, revealed for all times in Jesus Christ and tolerating no other gods besides. The church confesses its timidity, its deviations, its dangerous concessions ... It did not resist to the death the falling away from faith and is guilty of the godlessness of the masses . . ."[275]

This seems to me a chief sign of our intention to be a people of the truth. It is also a step toward building or re-building relationships with those with we seek to reach. And relationships are the most viable way to share the gospel in word and deed.

It cannot be stressed strongly enough, however, that evangelism through relationships is not a strategy. We are created for community, for relationships, for others. Befriending others is finally a matter of discovering our true humanity and co-humanity with others. Sharing life at this depth will offer many chances for us to bear winsome witness to our faith.

This dialogic process of befriending others is in itself a sign of the church's needed repentance. To make friends and get to know them in sufficient depth for such dialogue to occur is itself

---

275 Bonhoeffer, *Ethics*, 135-36.

a decision to reorder our lives. To prioritize time to be with and make new friends is a radical commitment for most of us. To step off the "mile wide and inch deep" carousel of our 24/7 wired and connected lives and order our time for a deeper and wider set of relationships is itself a gift of grace – and a counter-cultural one at that! It is the gift of what I call "lingering." Relationships don't just happen! We have to be available for them – that's what I mean by lingering.

Simple availability however is not enough. To availability must be added intentionality, what I call "listening." This is the gift of being present with others, giving them our attention, desiring to know who they are and what makes them tick. We are so full of ourselves – so many things to do, remember and think about – that we seldom give more than half-an-ear to others. To give full attention to another will mean that we empty ourselves, or rather, ask Jesus to empty us, and give us his heart for people.

Even availability and intentionality are not enough though. The final ingredient that transforms relationships with others into friendships that can be dialogic is vulnerability. I call this "listening." This is the gift of openness to being changed in relationship with someone else. Learning who they are, what they believe and seek to do, how they see the world and the like (what I earlier called priorities, passions, and practices) impact us and make us different people. Short of vulnerability, mutual vulnerability, friendships cannot form and community cannot develop, and the invitation to others to join Jesus' Counter-Revolutionary movement cannot be genuinely offered.

Dialogue, then, calls for an evangelism that is organic, relational, and centrifugal.

✓ Organic evangelism grows out of the day-to-day life of the people. It is not extrinsic to that life, a duty or obligation imposed by leaders or a special program, but an integral part of the rhythm of our life.

✓ Relational evangelism recognizes the dialogic nature of

sharing the good news with others. That invitation to faith must grow out of relationships within the community and relationships with those outside the community. We might even call this "sacramental" evangelism, in that these relationships, these friendships, mediate God's presence and power "face-to-face."

✓ Centrifugal evangelism seeks out others where they live and work and play. Centripetal evangelism, the "attractional" mode, the "build it and they will come" mentality, focuses on getting others to come to us, to our church. This has been the default form of evangelism in North America. Like the Counter-Revolutionaries we are, however, the church will spread out and in the context of our relationships with others share the good news with them where they are. Small groups of "Counter-Revolutionary" cells will thus spring up in various homes, neighborhoods, "third places,"[276] and even workplaces and form the nucleus for the church's ministry.

This is dialogue, the relational womb in which friendships grow, and evangelism can happen in winsome and timely ways.

Dignity and Destiny

Dignity is a second concern of evangelism to highlight. And it brings us to the theological heart of the different kind of evangelism I am advancing. The question I want to pose is: Who are the people we hope to evangelize? A seemingly simple question, to be sure. Yet one that has explosive power to shatter our theological misconceptions and help us reframe what we are doing when we share the gospel with others.

Here's another question: Do we have what I call a "Genesis 3 – Revelation 20" view of humanity or a "Genesis 1 and 2 – Rev-

---

276 "Third places" are social settings separate from home and work (our other two "places"). See Ray Oldenburg, *The Great Good Place: Cafes, Coffee Shops, Bookstores, Bars, Hair Salons, and Other Hangouts at the Heart of a Community* (De Capo Press, 1999).

elation 21 and 22" view? Are those with whom we share the gospel defined solely or primarily by sin or by their dignity as people created and called to be God's royal representatives who exercise care and oversight of God's creation? In other words, how do we consider the people who have not yet believed in Jesus and become a part of his Counter-Revolutionary people?

Traditional evangelism, working with a "shrunken" gospel, sees others as "Genesis 3 – Revelation 20" people. They are defined by sin - their lostness - and God's work, the atonement, is conceived solely as the antidote to this problem of human sin. Mix this conception with individualism and a transactional view of salvation (we must make the decision or pray the prayer to receive salvation) and you have the recipe for conventional evangelism.

If, however, we "unshrink" the gospel and view people in a full biblical perspective, what I called above "Genesis 1-2 and Revelation 21-22" people, a different way of seeing others emerges. What if human beings are not fully or primarily defined as sinners? What if humanity is best thought of under a more primal and comprehensive reality? What if we see others primarily as those created and called by God to be co-stewards and royal representatives of God's creation? Sin has catastrophically disrupted this relationship and twisted God's creation into a malignant anti-creation, a parody of God's handiwork, to be sure. But sin cannot destroy humanity's divine calling and mandate. It can only keep us from fulfilling it. Finding an antidote for sin, then, is only part of the good news we share with others. The full glory of the gospel is that God graciously gives us another chance to take up our primal roles as he designed and intended![277]

---

277 With characteristic vigor Karl Barth summarizes the theological underpinnings of this way of seeing others: "Man is no longer seriously regarded by God as a sinner. Whatever he may be, whatever there is to be said of him, whatever he has to reproach himself with, God no longer takes him seriously as a sinner. He has died to sin; there on the cross of Golgotha . . .the turn has been achieved once and for all." (cited in Mark Galli, "Love of Unimaginable Proportions," *Christianity Today*, March (Web only), 2010 at www.christianitytoday.com/ct/article_print.html?id=86920)

What does this mean for evangelism? Just this: to treat others as if they are fully defined by sin, as sinners, and therefore only in need of cleansing from sin, or forgiveness, is to say too little and to approach them on an inadequate basis. This is where the theology I have been developing gains traction and begins to work for us.

Dietrich Bonhoeffer points out the shortcomings of the "shrunken" gospel in evangelism. In a world "come of age," as Bonhoeffer put it, where humans live without need of or dependence on God, science and secularism have left God with only our "spiritual" needs to fix and "ultimate questions" of death and afterlife to answer (for example, "If you died tonight, where would you go?"). But, he warned,

> . . . if anyone has no such difficulties, or if he refuses to go into these things, to allow others to pity him, then either he cannot be open to God; or else he must be shown that he is, in fact, deeply involved in such problems, needs, and conflicts, without admitting or knowing it. If that can be done . . . then this man may now be claimed for God, and methodism[278] can celebrate its triumph. But if he cannot be brought to see and admit that his happiness is really an evil, his health sickness, and his vigor despair, the theologian is at his wits' end.[279]

Why is it that when we try and share the gospel with people whose lives are going well, whose families and financial lives are in good order, who are pillars of the community, and so on, that we find ourselves wondering just what we have to say to them? Or worse, if the gospel relates to their lives at all?

Bonhoeffer suggests the problem here is the assumption that we must see people only as sinners. We then have to ferret out their "weaknesses and meannesses"[280] to prove them such. Only then, we believe, our "shrunken" gospel can speak to them. However,

---

278 What we would call "evangelism"

279 Bonhoeffer, *Letters and Papers*, 341.

280 Bonhoeffer, *Letters and Papers*, 345. In a letter dated June 8 Bonheoffer calls this approach "pointless," "ignoble," and "unchristian" (*Letters and Papers*, 346).

when all that is apparent is that things are well with others, we have nothing to say to them in their "strength and success." Bonhoeffer, however, believes it is precisely at the point of their strengths and successes that God wants to address them.

Though he does not spell it out, I suspect Bonhoeffer is suggesting two things here. First, that our definition of "sin" is too small. This goes back to our insight that evangelism is about idolatry not morality. We are all, the weak and the immoral, the strong and the successful, idolaters. The gospel addresses each of us at the point of our idolatry, whether it be weakness or strength, and calls us to serve the "living and true God."[281]

Secondly, I believe Bonhoeffer is moving towards something similar to what I have suggested here – that there is a calling and vocation humanity is invited to re-embrace which forgiveness makes possible. If idolatry is our problem, that's a question of who we serve, who we are, and what we are to do with our lives. The gospel is God's gracious invitation to take up again our true and genuine identity and calling – the place of our real strength and success! Here it becomes apparent that which "gospel" we believe in makes all the difference!

How else can the gospel address humanity in its strength and success unless it calls us to our true destiny, a vocation of intrinsic worth and inestimable dignity. No recruit enters military service without flaws and rough edges that will be worked and trained out of them. But, few join the military just to have their flaws and rough edges corrected. Ideally they join because they sense the dignity and hear the call to serve their country resonate in their hearts and minds. Similarly, I suggest, the gospel stirs up in humanity a deep sense of dignity and destiny they have forfeited but is now offered as a free gift when Jesus' call to serve his Empire confronts them. Yes, they are sinners – make no mistake about that! And sin

---

281 1 Thessalonians 1:9. Bonhoeffer writes: "I therefore want to start from the premise that God shouldn't be smuggled into some last secret place, but that we should frankly recognize that the world, and people, have come of age, that we shouldn't run man down in his worldliness, but confront him at his strongest point" (*Letters and Papers*, 346).

needs to be taken care of. And it is. But if we come to Jesus simply to have our sin problem resolved, we miss out on the depth and significance of what has truly happened to us. And the results of such a "shrunken" gospel are apparent all around us. We see it in the cries of those who are outside of or leaving the church on account of its disconnect with their lives and overall lack of integrity. And it is apparent in the cry of Christian leadership throughout this country that there is a lamentable dearth of maturity in the churches of North America. It is apparent as well that an "unshrunk" version of the gospel is a necessity for evangelism in our world.

The dignity and destiny of human beings, even sinful human beings, is their call to serve creation and each other as God's representatives and stewards. The glory of redemption is their restoration to this primal glory and dignity. Let us never forget this as we share the good news of the gospel with the world.

Discernment

The third and final aspect of evangelism I am envisioning is discernment. This is a version of "truth in advertising." What does the gospel call people to be and do? Others need and deserve a fair and clear sense of what they're getting into when the gospel is offered to them. The analogy I have drawn between church and a Counter-Revolutionary movement is instructive here. The cost and consequences of involvement must be made as clear as possible or defection is inevitable. So too with the invitation to join Jesus' movement.

My friend and colleague David Batchelder has addressed this issue in regard to baptism. In an article entitled "Baptismal Renunciations: Making Promises We Do Not Intend to Keep,"[282] Batchelder argues that the ancient church's practice of making specific renunciations of various attitudes and practices inimical to the faith of those being baptized ought to be renewed. Further, he suggests we be very specific in naming attitudes and practices to be renounced. He offers as examples:

---

282 David Batchelder, "Baptismal Renunciations: Making Promises We Do Not Intend to Keep," *Worship* (2007), 409-25.

✓ Do you renounce all attempts to equate the Gospel of Christ with the American Dream?

✓ Do you renounce the power of the economy to define human value by what you consume and produce?

✓ Do you renounce the pursuit of national security at the expense of global security for this world God loves?

✓ Do you renounce all claims to national self-interest that privileges the prosperous over the poor, the comfortable over the suffering, and the powerful over the weak?

✓ Do you renounce all forms of puritanism which justify the practice of homophobia, sexism, racism, and a xenophobia that exploits immigrants and deprives them of justice?

✓ Do you renounce as false and demonic, all treatment of human beings whether the poor, victims of AIDS, detainees, or terrorists – that ignores their dignity as creatures made in the image of God?"

I suggest that evangelism ought to contain at least as specific a set of discernments of what the gospel calls God's people to be and do in their time and place. I've made a beginning by positing the image of church as the Counter-Revolutionary movement of God to reclaim, restore, and renew his creation, a creation that has been shanghaied by the powers of division, dehumanization, death, and destruction. I also made an analogy between baptism as the induction and boot camp processes of this Counter-Revolutionary movement and between Eucharist as the rations that nourish and energize "soldiers of Christ" throughout the struggle.

It is beyond the scope of this study to offer a comprehensive view of all that is entailed in following Jesus. But we can look again briefly at Jesus' Sermon on the Mount,[283] which we looked at earlier in Chapter 7. There we saw there that Jesus' sermon deals with the passions (5:12), the priorities (5:13-16), and the practices of God's Empire, God's Counter-Revolutionary movement. In summary,

---

283 Matthew 5-7.

✓ the passions of God's Empire are the search and struggle[284] for justice and peace – the right relations between everyone and everything in creation and the joy and harmony of that circumstance,

✓ the priorities of God's Empire are to be the public presence of God in the world, a sign of God's presence and a beacon of God's will and way for all creation ("salt" and "light," vv.13-16), and

✓ the practices of God's Empire – reconciliation, marital fidelity, truth-telling, love of enemy, care for the poor, prayer, fasting, serving God's Empire of peace and justice above all else, and trusting God rather than the empire.

That much, at least, ought to be made clear in any offer of the gospel. These, of course, are not human achievements but responses to the grace of God. But they are responses, ways we must seek to embody the call to follow Jesus in our time and place. This is the calling that befits the dignity of God's human creatures and these are the kinds of discernments that must be made to embody that calling.

Dialogue, dignity, and discernment – these are the elements, I believe, of an evangelism appropriate to both the "unshrunk" Gospel and the world in which we live. Let us turn our best efforts, then, to become communities of dialogue, dignity, and discernment. We might just turn the world upside down again!

---

284 "Blessed are those who hunger and thirst for righteousness . . ."(5:6)

AND NOW ... HOW WE EVANGELIZE AND WHAT WE CALL PEOPLE TO (PART 2)

Truth is so obscure in these times, and falsehood so established, that, unless we love the truth, we cannot know it.
– Blaise Pascal

RECAPPING THE SITUATION

Roberta Hestenes, pastor and former college president, was raised in a hardcore atheist home. Her parents forbade her to go to church. They ridiculed and dismissed any truth or value in the gospel story of Jesus. While in college, however, Hestenes was converted to Christ and began to seriously follow Jesus. When she told her father, he said, "How could this have happened? I thought we taught you better! You know, maybe I should have sent you to church after all. This probably would never have happened if we'd sent you to church as a child!"[285]

Lesslie Newbigin similarly has identified the effect of western Christianity as an inoculation of its people against the real thing.[286] That makes a fresh evangelism of our culture doubly difficult. Not only is it post-Christian in the sense Newbigin has described but it is post-pagan as well. That is, the neo-paganism of western culture today is not innocent of Christianity the way the paganism the gospel first encountered was. This calls for a radical re-thinking of evangelism in our time and place.

---

285 Recounted by Wes Avram, *Where the Light Shines Through: Discerning God in Everyday Life* (Grand Rapids: Brazos Press, 2005), 93.
286 See his full analysis in *Foolishness to the Greeks: The Gospel and Western Culture* (Grand Rapids: Wm. B. Eerdmans Publishing Co., 1986).

To that end I have re-visioned the church as God's Counter-Revolutionary movement to re-establish his rule over his world. We have explored Jesus and certain aspects of earliest Christianity to set the stage for this re-visioning. In the last chapter I laid out more fully how I see this evangelism incarnating itself in the day to day lives of Christian communities. The process has three aspects – dialogue in relationship with others, inviting them to join the Jesus' movement on the basis of their dignity as God's creatures called to be his royal representatives in, over, and with his creation rather than fundamentally as sinners, and discernments about the specific shape of God's Counter-Revolutionary movement in our time and place.

To this point we have focused on the contents of a gospel message for the church as God's Counter-Revolutionary movement to reclaim rule of his world. We have also seen that the fit between the medium (the church) and its message (the gospel) is essential to effective communication. In this final chapter we will explore this fit in more detail.

There is, of course, no one model or formula to follow here. The location and setting will have a substantial impact on the particular shape the church assumes and the specific discernments it makes about its life and ministry. The reflections here will thus inevitably remain somewhat general.

A Radical Alternative

If the situation of the church in North America is as I have styled it, and the biblical material does indeed point in the direction I have suggested, a radical new vision of church is needed to jolt us into action and thought that offers the world a genuine presence of the risen and living Christ.

Radical is surely the right word. Indeed, in his book Globo-Christ, Carl Raschke claims, "Christianity today must become far more radical than it has ever imagined."[287] I suspect many in our

---

287 Carl Raschke, *GloboChrist: The Great Commission Takes a Postmodern Turn* (Grand Rapids: Baker Academic, 2008), 114.

culture regard the word "radical" as chic buzzword and do not take it seriously. I intend it seriously, however, as does Raschke. So what might "radical" mean if we take it seriously?

In popular parlance "radical" suggests something "outside the box." If the church becomes more radical, then, its message and form will be something unexpected and unseen before in our culture. The gospel it preaches and the ministry it undertakes cannot be comprehended or contained in the present form and thought of what we have heretofore called "church." Radical as 'outside the box" is certainly a part of what I mean when I call for a radical church. "Radical" also carries with it an implicit and/or explicit critique of the status quo. And there has seldom if ever been a less status quo person than Jesus of Nazareth. As theologian William Placher writes, "If so radical a challenger of the status quo (as Jesus) is not crazy or possessed, then there must be something wrong with the status quo."[288] The people who follow Jesus, then, will embody an equally stringent critique of the status quo. This too is an aspect of the radical church we are called to be.

Finally, "radical" comes from the Latin radix which means going to the root. A radical approach to something, then, will dig to the roots or foundations in the interest of recovering or uncovering the original. My survey of the biblical material was designed in part to establish this aspect of the radicality of Jesus and his gospel.[289] My proposal to direct evangelism to the dignity and worth of human beings as God's creatures and stewards of his creation is likewise radical in that it cuts beneath the sin problem to recall us back to our original calling and vocation.

The church in our time and place, I submit must become radical in all these ways and more.

✓ "Outside the Box": because the present structuring of

---

288 William Placher, *The Triune God: An Essay in Postliberal Theology* (Louisville: Westminster John Knox Press, 2007), 66.

289 See Donald B. Kraybill, *The Upside-Down Empire* (Scottdale: Herald Press, 2003) for a comprehensive study of Jesus and the Empire of God along these lines.

the church militates against the church's transformation into a Counter-Revolutionary movement that is Mo-bile, Ag-ile, Host-ile, and Frag-ile!

✓ a Critique of the Status Quo: because the church is called to be a living demonstration of the Empire, its sign, sacrament, and steward. As such, the church necessarily critiques every other arrangement of social, political, and economic power because they all fall short of what God intends - mercy, justice, equality, and freedom for all, in short, the perfect freedom of serving the true and living God.

✓ Going to the Root: because the church must recover/ discover the form and dynamics of the Counter-Revolutionary movement of Jesus Christ, "as he is attested for us in Holy Scripture," the Jesus we trust and acclaim as "the one Word of God which we have to hear and which we have to trust and obey in life and in death."[290]

This radical church I am calling for arises from the depths of God's heart for his people and his world. In other words, the church is an act of God's love created to show that love in all its reality and radicality. It seems appropriate in that light to offer a few reflections on evangelism from Paul's great statement on love in 1 Corinthians 13.

LOVING THE TRUTH

Only love lasts. Only love finally matters. So says the Apostle Paul (1 Corinthians 13:8). Enduring testimony or witness, that is, evangelism, can only be an act of love. Love for God, love for the world, and especially with reference to evangelism, love of the truth, as Pascal notes. Communication of the gospel comes from communion with the truth (who is Jesus Christ himself!) and leads to communion with that same truth.

---

290 "The Theological Declaration of Barmen," *The Book of Confessions*, Presbyterian Church U.S.A. (Officce of the General Assembly), 8.11.

No evangelism, no matter how winsome, knowledgeable, charismatic, or sacrificial will endure or lead from communication to communion if it lacks love.[291]

Love for God, however, and for all that God loves, will season our evangelism so that it does indeed deepen our communication into communion with God and each other. Love seasons our communication, our evangelism, with community-builders and drives out community-busters. Patience, kindness, rejoicing in the truth, bearing, believing, hoping, and enduring all things; beyond all gifts and knowledge, fostering a maturity that leads us face-to-face with God – that is evangelism seasoned with love. Evangelism rooted in some other desire or passion inevitably exhibits the kind of things that so many rightly accuse the church of these days: impatience and envy, boastfulness and rude arrogance, a partisanship that seeks its own gain, an unseemly glee in the falling and failing of others, selectivity and exclusivity in its acceptance, enamored of gifts and certain kinds of knowledge, remaining immature and embroiled in childish ways, that does not and cannot open out into communion with God.[292]

Love, despite its domestication and dilution into a sentimental "Hallmark Card" staple, is a wild and boundless word. Love controls us, constantly "urging"[293] us to risk new ventures, move out beyond our comfort zones, even to ask where is the least likely place we believe Jesus would be present in our community and risk trying to find him there.

Love, untamed and untamable, names the passion[294] that animates the kind of evangelism I envision. Boundary breaking, border crossing, taboo crashing, treating what divides us from one another as doorways to fresh adventure, this is the kind of evan-

---

291 1 Corinthians 13:1-3.
292 1 Corinthians 13:4-13.
293 2 Corinthians 5:14.
294 Passion, as I am using it here, is similar to an "affection" as Jonathan Edwards uses that word in his classic *Religious Affections*. More than and deeper than a feeling, an affection is a disposition of one's being in a certain direction, a directed energy that moves us to action.

gelism I envision. Willing even to embrace the suffering sharing God's heart for his creation entails, the kind of suffering magnificently captured in G. A. Studdert-Kennedy's poem "The Suffering of God,"[295] which reads in part:

> *The sorrows o' God must be 'ard to bear*
> *If 'E really 'as Love in 'Is 'eart,*
> *And the 'ardest part i' the world to play*
> *Must surely be God's part.*

And this, this kind of evangelism begins right in our own homes and neighborhoods. This is incarnational love - love that takes root in the lives of those it lives with. This is incarnational love – love that makes itself vulnerable to the need and open to the gifts of those it lives with. This is incarnational love – love that is glocal (global + local). That is, this love brings the passion that brought the universe into being (global) into human lives (local) opening them anew to the world of human and ecological need which they are destined to oversee, care for, and protect. This is incarnational love – love that pours out[296] or lays down its life for others,[297] even its enemies.[298] This is incarnational love – love that is the "righteousness (that) exceeds that of the scribes and Pharisees" Jesus spoke of in the Sermon on the Mount.[299] This is incarnational love – the very love that God is[300] and we are called to become.[301] This is the love of the radical church I am calling God's Counter-Revolutionary movement. This is the love that constitutes the dignity for which we were created and for which we have been redeemed.

---

295 G. A. Studdert-Kennedy, *The Unutterable Beauty: The Collected Poems of G. A. Studdert-Kennedy* (London: Hodder and Stoughton, 1927), 131.
296 Philippians 2:17.
297 1 John 3:16.
298 Luke 23:34.
299 Matthew 5:20.
300 1 John 4:8.
301 1 John 4:19.

Practice of such love might almost make possible the well-known dictum attributed to St. Francis,[302] "Preach the Gospel at all times and when necessary use words." Almost, I say, because verbal announcement and explanation will always be needed, even with the most compelling demonstration of the gospel. God not only acted in Jesus, God also spoke in and through him the good news that could never be heard or found anywhere else!

A Sample of Counter-Revolutionary Transformation:
What Does It Mean to be Male?

Given the necessary generality of the last section I want to now provide a more concrete sample of the kind of people Jesus intends his Counter-Revolutionaries to become. If we can develop a profile of masculinity from Greco-Roman sources from the time of Jesus and the early church we can compare this to what the New Testament reveals about masculinity in light of the gospel and perhaps catch a glimpse of the difference following Jesus makes and the kind of transformation we might expect. I use masculinity for this survey because, unfortunately, we have more information about what Greco-Roman culture thought about being male than we have for females. This section is intended to illustrate the kind and degree of difference following Jesus makes for all his followers. The difference we can show for males should alert females that a similarly thorough-going transformation awaits them though we cannot demonstrate it in the same way given the present state of the evidence.

Greg Carey, in his recent book *Sinners: Jesus and His Earliest Followers*, harvests the growing research on traits of masculinity in the 1st century Greco-Roman world.[303] He details seven such traits.

---

302 See the discussion of this attribution at http://www.appleseeds.org/St-Fran_Preach-Gospel.htm

303 Greg Carey, *Sinners: Jesus and His Earliest Followers* (Waco: Baylor University Press, 2009, Chapter 4: "We Were Deadbeats, Me and Paul," 55-78.

To live in this world meant for men a life spent competing for honor (the top prize to attain in that world). Honor was a zero-sum matter. To gain more for oneself meant it came at the expense of someone else. Competition for honor, as you might well imagine, was intense. One's status in the social order and the power that goes with it was at stake.

Pursuit of honor and power for a Greco-Roman male entailed the following:

- ✓ physical vigor in military or athletic pursuits, but not manual labor;
- ✓ self-sufficiency
- ✓ outdoor life - the place of public and political life;
- ✓ accomplished oral skills;
- ✓ patronage: the acquisition and distribution of favors to distribute to others;
- ✓ marriage and children;
- ✓ self-control.

We have two main characters in the New Testament to compare and contrast with the Greco-Roman profile: Jesus himself and the Apostle Paul. We will look briefly at each in turn. Jesus, according to the gospels, shows overlap, redefinition, and conflict with this profile.

- ✓ Physical vigor is not dealt with directly in the gospels, though his labor involved in carpentry work would not be highly valued (overlap);
- ✓ Jesus rejects the ideal of self-sufficiency in a radical way; he teaches dependence in all things on God and he carries out his ministry depending on the goodwill and resources of those God moved to provide for him and his disciples (conflict);
- ✓ Jesus regularly engaged people outdoors, in the public, political sphere (overlap);
- ✓ Jesus possessed remarkable oral skills as his parables,

controversies with religious and other leaders, and his
words of power to heal and exorcise attest (overlap);

✓ Jesus had only the good news of God's Empire to offer
others and he never used access to this good news as a way
to oblige others or gain honor for himself; disciples were
free to enter the Empire and Jesus' band of followers and
to leave without debt or obligation (conflict);

✓ Jesus never married or had a natural family,[304] he
envisioned the possibility that natural family ties might
have to be surrendered out of loyalty to him, and he
redefined family in Empire of God terms rather than
blood (conflict and redefinition);

✓ Jesus exercised remarkable self-control (Gethsemane) but
never as a way to gain honor or power for himself in
relation to others; rather self-control was in the interest
of faithfulness and giving himself to God on a daily basis
(conflict and redefinition).

The Apostle Paul moved in more varied social settings than
did Jesus. A comparison of him with Greco-Roman traits of masculinity reveals, though, a similar pattern of overlap, redefinition,
and conflict.

✓ Paul gives physical vigor limited approval[305] and uses
military and athletic imagery but seems not to prize

---

304 Pace Dan Brown's claims otherwise in his blockbuster novel *The Da Vinci
Code*. Carey offers his analysis: "Some have protested that Jesus could
not have been single, let alone celibate, because any respectable rabbi
would marry, and if possible, father children. That argument does not
hold water; Jesus was not a rabbi in any technical sense, and our sources
concerning rabbis date from long after Jesus' career. Moreover, we possess
lots of evidence that some men, even religious devotees, pursued celibacy.
. . One wonders as well why Paul would encourage celibacy in 1 Corinthians 7, if that practice had no connection with Jesus himself. Simply,
the gospels portray a Jesus whose ministry is defined by travel and not by
household, who associates with women but does not marry" (64-65). See
further the recent work by Anthony LeDonne, *The Wife of Jesus: Ancient
Texts and Modern Scandals* (Oneworld Publications, 2013).
305 1 Timothy 4:8.

physical vigor in and of itself, though when he worked as a tentmaker he was engaged in the despised manual labor (conflict):

✓ like Jesus, Paul too rejects self-sufficiency as a positive character trait; and promotes giving his and our life over to God and God's will (conflict);

✓ Paul, again like Jesus, moves in the outdoor world of public affairs and politics (overlap);

✓ though capable of rhetorical power in his letters, Paul also sees himself as less skilled than his opponents, afflicted with some physical disability that would have counted against him in the public eye when it came to public speaking, and he regularly applauded God's penchant for expressing his power precisely through his own weakness (conflict):

✓ for Paul God was the great patron who gave gifts and honor and the one to whom we are indebted, though not because of his largesse but because of his free, unmerited grace (redefinition);

✓ Paul was most likely single, celibate, and without natural children; his "family" was the church in which he was both "father" and "mother";[306]

✓ as with Jesus, Paul also practices self-control, even listing it among the "fruit of the spirit"[307] but as a work of the Spirit he does not prize it as his own achievement nor does he seek to receive honor or power for its practice (conflict and redefinition)

Though there is some overlap between the Greco-Roman and Jesus-earliest Christian view of masculinity, the points of conflict and redefinition are more numerous and significant. It does appear that participation in the Empire of God deconstructs the Greco-Roman ideal and reconstructs a new framework within which

---

306 1 Thessalonians 2:7-12.
307 Galatians 5:22.

a "gospel" masculinity can be worked out afresh.[308] Carey concurs. He concludes that Jesus and the earliest Christians "did create space for men to consider themselves – and the other women, children, and men around them – differently."[309]

This particular evidence of the transforming power of the gospel of the Empire suggests, I believe, its potential to transform the whole of our life and relations with one another and the world. This kind of transformational power makes us into the Counter-Revolutionaries God created and redeemed us to be!

Practice Resurrection!

The last matter I want to lift up in sketching something of the ethos and experience of belonging to God's Counter-Revolutionary movement, the church, is resurrection. Love, as we saw, is the radicalism of this movement. And it expressed itself in the most radical way possible: Jesus' resurrection from the dead!

Jesus' resurrection is the foundation and bedrock of Christian faith. Simply put, no resurrection, no Christianity! If resurrection, whole new world! To quote St. Paul again, "If anyone be in Christ – new creation. Old things have gone, but note, new things have come to stay!"[310] And that's what I want to pick up on here. Jesus' resurrection from the dead nullifies every definition of reality that disallows or disregards it and makes it mandatory for Jesus' followers to open their hearts and minds to its new reality.

Yet this seems one of the most difficult things for us to do. In my experience, both personal and pastoral, we cling like grim death to old ways and old perspectives. "We've never done it that way before" is one infamous expression of this reluctance or in-

---

308 That such a task still lies in our future is suggested by the eager embrace and imposition of a secular patriarchal view of masculinity, marriage, and fatherhood, euphemistically called "family values," as well as the recent movement to use Mixed Martial Arts as an outreach tool to young males and to invest Jesus with machismo. See the article by James Michael-Smith at http://www.examiner.com/examiner/x-8276-Methodist-Examiner-y2010m2d4-Ultimate-FightingJesus#.

309 Carey, Sinners, 78.

310 2 Corinthians 5:17, my translation.

ability. Another way to identify this malady is what I call the "Yes, But" syndrome. This occurs whenever we find ourselves reading Scripture or considering a teaching of the New Testament and find ourselves thinking, "Yes, that's likely true" or "Yes, I really should do that, BUT (for reasons usually grounded in old perceptions of "reality") I just can't risk it", or "Nobody will believe me," or "I can't do it," or "I don't want to do it."[311] I suspect that, like me, dear readers, most of you have "Yes, But–ed" God on more than a few occasions.

Finding our way out of the cramped confines of assumptions about reality now nullified by Jesus' resurrection from the dead and learning to live in the open skies and broad fields of resurrection freedom is the life source of God's Counter-Revolutionary movement. "Practice resurrection," then, is the order of the day for God's people. And no one has described this reality better in brief compass than Christian-Farmer-philosopher-social critic Wendell Berry in his poem "Practice Resurrection."[312]

> *Love the quick profit, the annual raise,*
> *vacation with pay. Want more*
> *of everything ready-made. Be afraid*
> *to know your neighbors and to die. . .*
>
> .
>
> *So, friends, every day do something*
> *that won't compute. Love the Lord.*
> *Love the world. Work for nothing. . .*
> *Practice resurrection!*

What makes practicing resurrection more than a quixotic tilting at windmills? Why, Jesus' resurrection of course! In this event we see a man "practice resurrection" throughout his life, even surrendering his life to do it. And we have also seen that life validated

---

311 The classic biblical example is Moses attempts to evade God's call to go to Pharaoh in Exodus 3 – 4.

312 Wendell Berry, "Practice Resurrection" at http://www.context.org/ICLIB/IC30/Berry.htm. The complete poem is available on that site.

and vindicated by God as the way he wants his people to live in this fallen world through his mighty act of raising Jesus from the grave!

So practice resurrection, indeed! Radical love, ongoing transformation, resurrection reality and hope - such is the life of Counter-Revolutionaries God calls to assist in his subversion of the powers of evil, death, and the devil and re-establish his rule over the world.

Incarnation, love, resurrection power, radical witness, congruent lifestyle – this is the life of Jesus lived by his people. It is also . . . evangelism!

POSTSCRIPT

I have cast the church in the image of God's Counter-Revolutionary movement called by God to implement the victory of Jesus Christ as a means of re-establishing and extending God's rightful rule over all creation. This non-violent struggle, carried out by the Word of God and the "violence of love" captures a vision of church more commensurate with both God's original intent in creation and the rescue mission God undertook when his creatures went astray. For the former, we were always to be God's royal representatives in creation, nurturing it to maturity and protecting it for maturity. We might call humanity at this stage God's "Bearers of Creation's Destiny." For the latter, after the fall into sin, those who ally themselves with God through faith in Christ are his "Bearers of Creation's Redemption." This corps of folk, those we call the church, are necessarily in conflict with those who remain wedded to sin and its pursuits along with their demonic overlords as they seek to restore God's original creative plan.

Often overlooked is that the latter, "God's Bearers of Creation's Redemption," ultimately serve the interests of the former group, "God's Bearers of Creation's Destiny." Creation and Redemption are inextricably linked. God's saves his human creatures that they may be restored to their original vocation of bearing creation's destiny. They henceforth engage in the struggle, God's struggle, to reclaim, renew, restore, and replenish his creation to its intended destiny. God's saving work does not return us to the Garden of Eden, or worse, spirit us off to some immaterial, "spiritual" life we are prone to call "heaven." Rather God restores us to our original vocation of bearing creation's destiny, on the way to the holy city, the New Jerusalem. In this city the original garden is present in the symbols of the tree and river of life.[313] However the garden now sits amidst the great new city, the New Jerusalem, creation's destiny.

The conflict we engage in is what I have called "counter-revolutionary." The fall into sin is the first revolution or rebellion against God, the world's rightful ruler. Ousted from his throne, as it were, God initiates a counter-revolution through Abraham and his family to reclaim his rule and his creatures. From that moment on, the people of Abraham, the people of Christ, Abraham's one faithful son, are counter-revolutionaries in the service of the "exiled" God and serve as this God's "beachhead" in enemy territory for conducting the counter-revolution.

This image of the church as a "Counter-Revolutionary" movement suggests a new and different sense of identity for Christians and the church. It points to changes in the way the church functions as well. Counter-Revolutions require small, committed groups of highly trained people who seek to retake their ultimate object one day at a time. Counter-Revolutionaries seek to establish new cells of subversive resistance every place they go. They are always on the move. Continuous training of both new recruits and veterans is top priority. Revolutionaries are in the struggle for the long haul and, regardless of personal differences, are committed to having each other's back no matter the cost. The focus is on the work to be done, not the gatherings required for strategizing and debriefing. These gatherings are necessary, essential even, but they are not the goal. They anticipate that goal, prefigure it, even offer a provisional experience of the goal, but they are not the final embodiment or full experience of that goal. That glory always lies ahead of us as long as we journey on.

---

313 Revelation 22:1-2.

The particular character of God's "Counter-Revolution" is defined by the reality that the war, the "Counter-Revolution," is already won (as we saw in an earlier chapter). We wage our counter-revolution certain that victory is and will be ours. We are, as it were, the troops who carry out the implementation of God's victory through Jesus' death and resurrection (the "mop up" crew). We struggle to identify and root out pockets of resistance that continue on even though their struggle is futile. Much like the Allied forces between D-Day and V-Day in World War II, the battles still rage though the war is decided. The Allied troops, therefore, had to remain alert and battle-ready till such time as the fighting actually ceased. So too for us. It is not ours to rest now; that will come later. But for now our call is take up and put on God's armor[314] and join the fray in the confident and strong hope given us by Jesus Christ himself.

Evangelism in a Counter-Revolutionary church is its daily communication with its world. It is a mistake to treat evangelism as a discrete activity. Lives formed by the worship, work, and daily life together of these "spore"-like cells of believers carry maximal weight evangelistically. Evangelism includes everything we do and the way we do it. For this communicates best what we truly believe and value. Critics who point to the "disconnect" that drives them away from the church are often responding to the lack of just this kind of witness.

Even though the Spirit gifts the church with particular people who have passion and aptitude for evangelism in the sense of declaring the message to others in persuasive and winsome ways, the declaration of the gospel is also a responsibility of every believer. That unfortunately causes both guilt and anxiety in our churches because by and large we do not do and do not really want to do evangelism as we understand it. Those in a Counter-Revolutionary church such as I envision would experience the sharing of faith and the gospel as a seamless, organic part of their life rather than an

---

314 Ephesians 6:10-20.

"add-on" or extrinsic duty that sits clumsily or discordantly with the tone and tenor of the rest of our lives.

A chief reason for this organic feel to evangelism is that the act of belonging to this church entails a sense of self and world and a commitment to a vision that prioritizes the living out and spreading of the (biblical) gospel. Our lives and perspectives grow increasingly "Counter-Revolutionary" so that we more and more see and experience life through that lens. Sharing our faith and gospel with others will not feel like doing something different from what we usually do. Rather, such witness will flow naturally in the give and take of relationships and conversations. At any time such relationships and conversations may present us with a chance to articulate what our lives are about and why – and we will not experience discomfort in bearing that witness.

That, baldly stated, is a summary of the "Gospel Unshrunk" and the difference I believe it makes for evangelism. I want to end on another note altogether, though.

In the introduction we looked at van Gogh's famous painting *Starry Night*. We observed that of all the buildings in the painting only the church building was without the light of God's life and love. That became our leading image for the disconnect many, including van Gogh himself, experience between the church's profession and its life.

I want us to look at *Starry Night* again now at the end of our journey. I think we may see it with different eyes and find it an image, now not for our disconnect with others, but a new way ahead as God's Counter-Revolutionary movement.

    As I look again at this painting it strikes me that perhaps, in light of an "unshrunk" Gospel, it is just as powerful an image for the new way of being church I have outlined. Maybe it's right that the life and light of God are not holed up in the church house but out in the community illumining homes, meeting centers, businesses, schools, and so on. Maybe that's where the church should be, in those homes, meeting centers, and schools. Maybe that's where the work of evangelism, the recruiting of new members for God's Counter-Revolutionary movement best takes place. Maybe this sharing of life as it is with people where they are will bring us together with them under the love of God made known in Jesus Christ. Perhaps we will be able together to learn to see the starry night again as God's creation, ourselves as those divinely beloved even in our sin and rebellion, rescued and called anew to be the caretakers and protectors of this wondrous planet for and with God forever.

My final word for God's Counter-Revolutionary movement is a blessing, a Jesuit benediction, I believe. It captures perfectly the calling and hope of such a people:

May God bless us with distress at easy answers, half-truths, and superficial relationships, so that we may live from deep within our hearts.

May God bless us with pain over the hurt and anguish of others, that we may stretch forth our hands to bring comfort and turn their pain into joy.

May God bless us with anger at injustice, oppression, and exploitation of others, so that we may stretch forth our hands to do justice and make peace.

May God bless us with foolishness, foolishness enough to believe that we can make a difference, thus doing what others claim cannot be done. Amen.

The Jesus Paradigm

David Alan Black

Few readers will appreciate all aspects of Black's argument, but it is high time we all heard and heeded its radical, sobering, and exciting call to the Church of Jesus Christ simply to obey her Master!

Richard J. Erickson
Associate Professor of
New Testament
Fuller Theological Seminary

This text is profound without being preachy, and inspires the reader to claim a faith that is adventurous and world-changing. One of the best presentations of the progressive Christian vision I have read.

Bruce Epperly, PhD
Author of *Process Theology: Embracing Adventure with God* and *A Center in the Cyclone: Twenty-first Century Clergy Self-care*

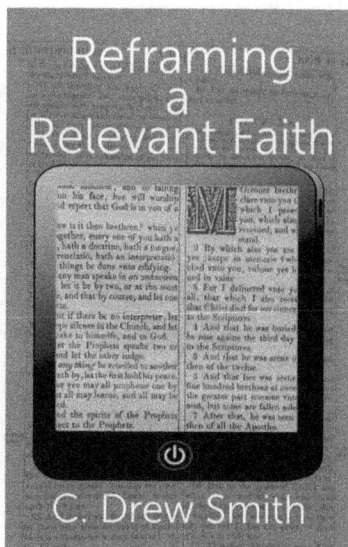

Reframing a Relevant Faith

C. Drew Smith

MORE FROM ENERGION PUBLICATIONS

Personal Study

Holy Smoke! Unholy Fire	Bob McKibben	$14.99
The Jesus Paradigm	David Alan Black	$17.99
When People Speak for God	Henry Neufeld	$17.99
The Sacred Journey	Chris Surber	$11.99

Christian Living

It's All Greek to Me	David Alan Black	$3.99
Grief: Finding the Candle of Light	Jody Neufeld	$8.99
My Life Story	Becky Lynn Black	$14.99
Crossing the Street	Robert LaRochelle	$16.99
Life as Pilgrimage	David Moffett-Moore	14.99

Bible Study

Learning and Living Scripture	Lentz/Neufeld	$12.99
From Inspiration to Understanding	Edward W. H. Vick	$24.99
Philippians: A Participatory Study Guide	Bruce Epperly	$9.99
Ephesians: A Participatory Study Guide	Robert D. Cornwall	$9.99
Ecclesiastes: A Participatory Study Guide	Russell Meek	$9.99

Theology

Creation in Scripture	Herold Weiss	$12.99
Creation: the Christian Doctrine	Edward W. H. Vick	$12.99
The Politics of Witness	Allan R. Bevere	$9.99
Ultimate Allegiance	Robert D. Cornwall	$9.99
History and Christian Faith	Edward W. H. Vick	$9.99
The Journey to the Undiscovered Country	William Powell Tuck	$9.99
Process Theology	Bruce G. Epperly	$4.99

Ministry

Clergy Table Talk	Kent Ira Groff	$9.99
Out of This World	Darren McClellan	$24.99

Generous Quantity Discounts Available
Dealer Inquiries Welcome
Energion Publications — P.O. Box 841
Gonzalez, FL 32560
Website: http://energionpubs.com
Phone: (850) 525-3916

www.ingramcontent.com/pod-product-compliance
Lightning Source LLC
Chambersburg PA
CBHW022129080426
42734CB00006B/281